ASHLAND

000427363

Jackson County Library System
Medford, OR 97501

WITHDRAWN
Damaged, Obsolete, or Surplus

Jackson County Library Services

FOR REFERENCE
Do Not Take From This Room

ASHLAND PUBLIC LIBRARY
ASHLAND, OREGON 97520

NOV 6 '92

THE VIETNAM WAR
The Tet Offensive Onward

The
MILITARY HISTORY
of the
UNITED STATES

Christopher Chant

THE VIETNAM WAR
The Tet Offensive Onward

MARSHALL CAVENDISH
NEW YORK · LONDON · TORONTO · SYDNEY

NOV 6 '92

ASHLAND PUBLIC LIBRARY
ASHLAND, OREGON 97520

JACKSON COUNTY LIBRARY SYSTEM
MEDFORD, OREGON 97501

Library Edition Published 1992

© Marshall Cavendish Limited 1992

Published by
Marshall Cavendish Corporation
2415 Jerusalem Avenue
PO Box 587
North Bellmore
New York 11710

All rights reserved. No part of this book may be reproduced or utilized
in any form or by any means electronic or mechanical
including photocopying, recording, or by any information storage
and retrieval system, without permission from the copyright holders.

Series created by Graham Beehag Book Design

Series Editor	Maggi McCormick
Consultant Editors	James R. Arnold
	Roberta Wiener
Sub Editor	Julie Cairns
Designer	Graham Beehag
Illustrators	John Batchelor
	Steve Lucas
	Terry Forest
	Colette Brownrigg
Indexer	Mark Dartford

The publishers wish to thank the following organizations
who have supplied photographs:

The National Archives, Washington. United States
Navy, United States Marines, United States Army,
United States Air Force, Department of Defense,
Library of Congress, The Smithsonian Institution.

The publishers gratefully thank the U.S. Army Military
History Institute, Carlisle Barracks, PA. for the use of
archive material for the following witness accounts:

Page 67
*Aces & Aerial Victories: The United States Air Force in
Southeast Asia 1965-1972* by Frank Futerell
Office of Air Force History, Headquarters U.S. Air
Force, 1976.

Page 84
Medal of Honor citation for Jack H. Jacobs.
From *Vietnam Era Medal of Honor Recipients*
Committee on Veterans Affairs, U.S. Senate, 93rd
Congress, 1st session. (U.S. Government Printing
Office, Washington, 1973).

Vietnam History of the Bulwark B-2 Theater
by Tran Fan Tra (Washington, 1968).

Library of Congress Cataloging-in-Publication Data

Chant, Christopher.
    The Military History of the United States / Christopher Chant –
Library ed.
        p. cm.
    Includes bibliographical references and index.
    Summary: Surveys the wars that have directly influenced the
    United States., from the Revolutionary War through the Cold War.
    ISBN 1-85435-364-0 ISBN 1-85435-361-9 (set)
    1. United States - History, Military - Juvenile literature.
    [1. United States - History, Military.] 1. Title.
    t181.C52 1991
    973 - dc20   90 - 19547
                                                         CIP
                                                         AC

Printed in Singapore by Times Offset PTE Ltd
Bound in the United States

Contents

During the fall of 1967, Secretary of Defense Robert McNamara indicated to President Lyndon B. Johnson that there was "a very real question whether ... it will be possible to maintain our efforts in South Vietnam for the time necessary to accomplish our objectives there." The two most obvious solutions were an increase in American combat forces to South Vietnam and a strengthening of the bombing of North Vietnam in an effort to force the communists to the negotiating table, but the growing hostility of the American people to the war made either solution equally unlikely. This deepening public opposition to the war grew out of the worsening casualty rate, the adverse effect of the war on the domestic economy, and the perception of many Americans that the administration and the military were not telling the real truth about the situation in Southeast Asia.

With all these factors in mind, McNamara suggested that the only other solution was to stop the bombing of North Vietnam and announce that there would be no further increase in the size of the U.S. commitment to South Vietnam. McNamara hoped that the pressure of world opinion produced by such announcements would force the communists to the negotiating table. If the United States also scaled down its land operations in South Vietnam to the minimum necessary for security, the scale of American casualties would be reduced, and the men and materiel needed to boost the training and thus the fighting capabilities of a strengthened South Vietnamese army would be available.

McNamara's suggestion caused a considerable stir in Washington. The Department of Defense rejected it, but a considerable number of senior figures in the Johnson administration favored it. Johnson did nothing, and it was clear from this time forward that there was a basic split within the administration

With its ventral airbrake extended to keep speed in check, a North American F-100 Super Sabre fighter of the 481st Tactical Fighter Squadron makes a strafing attack on Viet Cong positions. Too old for continued service as a first-line fighter, the Super Sabre proved very successful in the Vietnam War as a fighter-bomber for the ground-attack role.

Much of the feel of the Vietnam War is conveyed by this photograph of a marine belonging to Company "E," 2nd Battalion, 3rd Marine Regiment, 3rd Marine Division, on Mutters Ridge near the Demilitarized Zone north of Dong Ha during Operation "Lancaster II" in 1968.

Dien Bien Phu
For further references see pages
10, 21

about the way the war should be conducted.

Similar American and North Vietnamese Conclusions

By one of the ironic twists of fate that seem to bedevil history, the communist leadership of North Vietnam was also considering the course of the war and reaching similar conclusions: matters were not going well. In the communist camp, however, the problem was purely a military one: the present strategy was securing no real gains, but resulting in a very heavy casualty rate. In 1954, the communists had secured a decisive advantage over the French with a careful coordination of diplomatic and military strategies that came together with the victory at Dien Bien Phu. What was needed now, the communist leadership decided, was a second Dien Bien Phu to score a major military success over the U.S. forces in South Vietnam and deal a

Men of SEAL Team One move down the Bassac River in a STAB (SEAL Team Assault Boat) during operations south of Saigon. The SEAL (Sea, Air, and Land) unit, the navy's equivalent of the U.S. Army Special Forces, proved itself highly capable during the course of the Vietnam War.

William C. Westmoreland
For further references see pages
11, 13, 14, *16*, 20, 22, 23, 24, 39

major psychological blow to the United States itself.

In July 1967, the North Vietnamese leadership recalled its diplomats from various parts of the world to analyze the current situation and recommend future policy. Under the direct supervision of the communist leader, Ho Chi Minh, and the armed forces' commander in chief, General Vo Nguyen Giap, the North Vietnamese leadership arrived at what General William C. Westmoreland, commander of the U.S. Military Assistance Command, Vietnam, rightly called "a crucial decision regarding the conduct of the war." The large-scale, coordinated effort was described to field commanders as the decisive communist effort to end the war. North Vietnam would attempt to topple the South Vietnamese regime of President Nguyen Van Thieu and Vice President Nguyen Cao Ky through a combination of direct military effort and insurrection. Viet Cong and North Vietnamese army forces would attack throughout South Vietnam to capture the main towns and cities; and

communist cadres in South Vietnam would rise and, with the aid of local sympathizers, take over the government at local level, thereby overthrowing the current government.

Mixed Motives

The North Vietnamese had high hopes for the planned offensive, but probably not in the form revealed to the field commanders. It is more likely that the communists hoped to secure considerable, although perhaps not decisive, military advantage in South Vietnam; more importantly, they expected to win a huge psychological victory. The North Vietnamese knew full well that in the United States the emotional, moral, and intellectual tide was beginning to turn against the war in a year that would see an important presidential election. They therefore planned their major offensive to inflict catastrophic losses on the Americans and South Vietnamese to show ordinary Americans citizens that the South Viet-

The side-door gunner in a Bell UH-1 utility helicopter of the 1st Marine Air Wing searches the terrain beside him for communist targets. The task of the gunner and his 7.62-mm (0.3-inch) caliber pintle-mounted M60 machine gun was to find and kill any opposition that could interfere with air-mobility helicopters moving into and out of their tactical landing zones.

namese were incapable of defeating or even checking the communists by themselves. This might lead to the election of a president committed to a U.S. withdrawal from Southeast Asia on the basis of a negotiated settlement that would favor the communists.

As in every military undertaking, the key to success was total tactical and operational surprise. After careful consideration, the North Vietnamese leadership decided to launch the offensive on the eve of the Tet holiday, the Vietnamese celebration of the lunar new year. In 1789, such a plan had resulted in the ousting of the Chinese from Hanoi. Comparable success was expected from the 1978 offensive, for the Viet Cong had already declared that they would observe a truce in the Tet period between January 27 and February 3. The Tet holiday has greater importance in the Vietnamese calendar than virtually any similar celebration in

the Western calendar, and to make sure that their own people enjoyed Tet, the North Vietnamese brought the holiday forward to begin on January 27. This meant that North Vietnam would have three days of Tet celebrations before the offensive was launched late on the night of January 30-31, the real beginning of the Tet celebrations.

The North Vietnamese had already shown enormous skill in the slow massing of forces and equipment in South Vietnam in spite of air attacks north and south of the Demilitarized Zone. They now wanted to secure a further edge by persuading the Americans to end, or at least to pause, their air campaign against North Vietnam. North Vietnam therefore used roundabout diplomatic channels to inform the United States that if it halted bombing, North Vietnam would participate in talks to end the war. In previous moves, the North Vietnamese

9

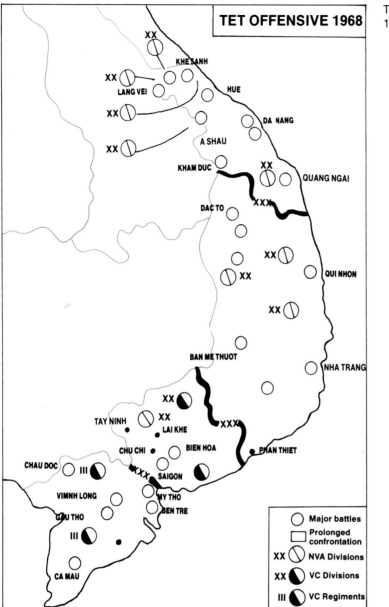

TET OFFENSIVE 1968

Major battles

Prolonged confrontation

XX **NVA Divisions**

XX **VC Divisions**

III **VC Regiments**

The Tet Offensive 1968.

had only hinted at attending talks in exchange for a bombing pause, so this was seen in Washington as a real advance. In mid-January 1967, therefore, the U.S. passed the message to the North Vietnamese that it would demonstrate good faith by ending the bombing around Hanoi. It was not as much as the North Vietnamese had hoped, but it helped in the preparation of the offensive.

Harassment South of the Demilitarized Zone

Another part of the North Vietnamese deception was to continue attacks against American positions just to the south of the Demilitarized Zone. By the end of 1967, such border battles had been fought at Song Be, Loc Ninh, and Dak To. Another feint, (although one of which more was expected) was the siege of the U.S. fire support base at Khe Sanh. The North Vietnamese hoped that the severity of the attacks there would persuade the U.S. that the communists saw the battle as another Dien Bien Phu. By mid-January 1968, the communists had concentrated large numbers of men and considerable quantities of materiel, especially artillery, on the approaches to

Hanoi
For further references
see pages
9, 11, 61

Khe Sanh
For further references
see pages
11, 21, 22, 25, 27, 28,
29, 31, 36, 37, 38, 51,
83, 85, 86, 88

Khe Sanh. The siege of Khe Sanh was launched on January 21 with a heavy bombardment by rocket launchers, mortars, and artillery.

Westmoreland and other U.S. commanders suspected that the communists might be planning a surprise move for the Tet period, and as the festivities approached, this disquiet spread to some of the more able South Vietnamese commanders. Westmoreland persuaded a reluctant Thieu to guarantee that at least half of the Army of the Republic of Vietnam (A.R.V.N.) was on standby during the holiday, to cancel the ceasefire in the northern provinces, and to shorten the ceasefire in other areas to just 24 hours. Thieu clearly did not seriously believe that a communist offensive was close, for he left Saigon to spend the holiday with his wife's family in the Mekong Delta.

Other South Vietnamese officers were less short-sighted. Several refused to grant their men leave, among them the commanders of two units near Saigon, one in the central highlands, and one in the city of Hue.

By late January, the communist plan was ready. Its object was a wide-ranging offensive by Viet Cong and North Vietnamese units on cities and military installations throughout South Vietnam designed to destroy South Vietnam's military capabilities and persuade the civilian population to overthrow the current regime. 80,000 or more communist troops were under arms in South Vietnam.

The communist order of battle included nine North Vietnamese army divisions, two Viet Cong divisions, and two Viet Cong regiments. Eight of the North Vietnamese divisions operated in the northern two-thirds of the country, while the ninth supported the Viet Cong in the southern third.

The Element of Total Surprise is Lost

Despite the careful planning of the offensive in Hanoi, for some still-unexplained reason, part of the operation was launched a day early when, late on the night of January 29-30, communist forces attacked eight towns and cities in

Men of the 3rd Marine Regiment hurl grenades at suspected communist positions. Even when these weapons did not actually kill or wound the enemy, the blast of their detonation partially stunned the communists and gave the attackers a brief but important tactical advantage as they moved into the assault.

Nguyen Van Thieu
For further references see pages
8, 13, 17, 40, 55, 75, 76, 77, 81, 124, 127, 129, 131

Right: Throughout the war, the Viet Cong and North Vietnamese were well briefed on allied dispositions and weapons. These aircraft identification and information sheets were captured from the Viet Cong.

Below: Men of III Marine Amphibious Force wait in their positions around the village of Namo for a communist attack during the Tet offensive of February 1968.

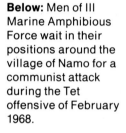

THE VIETNAM WAR – THE TET OFFENSIVE ONWARD

The power of the Bell UH-1 in the defense-suppression role was considerably boosted by the adoption of a lightweight launcher for seven 2·75-inch (70-mm) caliber air-to-surface rockets. Carried as one seven-round launcher on each side of the fuselage, the rocket system was aligned to fire along the helicopter's line of flight and was controlled by the pilot.

the central highlands and in the central part of the coastal provinces. Battalion-strength attacks were committed against Nha Trang, Hoi An, and Ban Me Thuot, two battalions attacked Qui Nhon, a sapper (combat engineer) assault was delivered against the headquarters of the South Vietnamese I Corps in Da Nang, and other attacks were made against Pleiku and a distant provincial capital.

With their suspicions already aroused, U.S. and South Vietnamese commanders saw these attacks not as a single episode but as a warning of major events to come. Thus the early start in this area, which lay in the operational zone of a single North Vietnamese army command,

provided a useful though short warning. As Major General Phillip B. Davidson, Westmoreland's intelligence chief, put it: "This is going to happen in the rest of the country tonight or tomorrow morning." Soon after daylight, Thieu cancelled the ceasefire and alerted all South Vietnamese forces, though it was too late to recall troops who had already departed on leave. American units all over South Vietnam were also put on full alert.

It was also too late to try to intercept the small parties of Viet Cong and North Vietnamese who had taken advantage of the relaxed feeling of the past few days to move into their operational areas disguised in civilian clothes as some of the

This hole was blown through the wall surrounding the U.S. embassy in Saigon by the small communist assault force at the beginning of the Tet offensive.

many hundreds of thousands of holiday travelers.

When the main part of the Tet offensive started on time, one small episode, an attack by 15 "suicide" sappers on the American embassy in Saigon, only a short distance from the presidential palace and the major hotels used by the large corps of foreign media, was destined to exercise a wholly disproportionate importance of subsequent events.

A Minor Episode Becomes a Major Issue

The embassy was a modern building of reinforced construction surrounded by a sturdy perimeter wall. Before daybreak on January 31, the Viet Cong party blew a hole through the perimeter and stormed through the breach. The first two Viet Cong were killed by two military policemen on duty in the area, but these two men were also killed in the exchange of fire as the rest of the Viet Cong pushed through toward the main building. Two more military policemen and a marine sniper were killed: the military policemen had arrived by jeep after the first blast, and the marine had climbed onto a

nearby building so that he could fire down on the Viet Cong in the embassy compound. Before the Viet Cong could reach and enter the chancery building, its doors were closed and locked by another military policeman. The Viet Cong party was now trapped between the chancery and the perimeter wall, and in the following six hours, all were killed by fire from an orbiting helicopter and a platoon of airborne soldiers lifted by helicopter onto the roof of the chancery.

The fire fight inevitably attracted the attention of the media people in nearby hotels. Arriving while it was still dark, some decided that the Viet Cong had broken into the chancery and reported this as fact. The American public was deeply shocked by the "news," and even after Westmoreland had toured the building and reported that the Viet Cong had not broken in, the media continued to claim that "other sources" reported that the Viet Cong had entered the building. On a military level, whether or not the Viet Cong had entered the chancery was wholly irrelevant. At the psychological level, however, the episode was profoundly important. The media was now more firmly convinced than ever that encouraging war news pumped out

Sergeant, Infantry, U.S. Army, Vietnam, 1968

Infantry units of several types bore the brunt of the fighting for the American force throughout the Vietnam War, and this infantry sergeant is typical of the American soldier at the height of U.S. involvement in South Vietnam. The core of his uniform is a cotton jungle utility suit, which became standard in late 1965 and early 1966. It had distinctive bellows pockets on the jacket. The earlier style had exposed buttons on the pockets and shoulder straps; the later one had flaps over the buttons and was made of ripstop fabric, in which nylon filaments were woven into the cotton. The man's boots are of the rubber-and-leather jungle type. The earlier style of this footwear had buckles at the ankle that were unpopular because they were uncomfortable and wore badly. The much superior later boots had a nylon reinforcement at the ankle and an aluminum insole for protection against *punji* spikes. The helmet is the M1 type with a camouflaged cover, and it sports a section of rubber inner tube as a band that could be used to carry items such as a field dressing. The weapon is the 5.56-mm (0.22-inch) caliber M16A1 assault rifle, with extra ammunition magazines carried in the pouches of the cotton bandolier. The other major item of kit is the M1967 Modernized Load-Carrying Equipment carrying a knife bayonet and M18 smoke grenades.

General William C. Westmoreland visits the U.S. embassy after the end of the communist attack. It was a symptom of the acute breakdown in relations between the military and the media that the latter refused to accept the general's categorical assertion that there were no live attackers still inside the building.

by the administration had at best shaded the truth, and at worst told downright falsehoods. Because the media disseminated this point of view, it began to color the thinking of the American public toward a belief that the direction of the war was in fact far worse than they had been told. If the Viet Cong could fight their way into an American embassy, the average American began to wonder, could there really be truth in a recent claim ''that the end begins to come into view''?

Appalling InterAmerican Relations

The previously poor relations between the military and the media now veered toward the antagonistic. For too long, reports of military successes had included large body counts of communist dead, and the media was no longer prepared to believe these patently exaggerated figures. The

military's inability to secure a favorable press came home to roost with a vengeance, and after the Tet offensive, the American media began to question virtually everything reported by the military. Since media reports were a major factor in molding the thinking of the average American, the Tet offensive can without a doubt be claimed as the major turning point in the war: from then on, the American public increasingly distrusted what the military and the administration told them. This, then, was the great success for which the North Vietnamese had planned their offensive.

In other parts of Saigon, there were five other attacks by small sapper units. One group of North Vietnamese in South Vietnamese uniform tried to storm the presidential palace, but was driven back. Battalion-sized units occupied a cemetery and a racetrack, but were soon defeated by South Vietnamese units. Potentially more damaging attacks were delivered against Tan Son Nhut Airport and the headquarters of the South Vietnamese Joint General Staff, but were also defeated. The communists had relatively little military success in Saigon: Thieu declared a state of martial law on January 31, but was able to lift it on February 5, when Saigon was troubled by only a few small, isolated communist units.

As the situation in Saigon was brought under control, reports from the rest of South Vietnam began to reveal the scope of the communist undertaking. In overall terms, they had made infantry and/or mortar and rocket attacks on 36 out of 44 provincial capitals, five out of six autonomous cities, 64 out of 242 district capitals, 50 hamlets, and 23 airfields and other bases. The largest attacks were directed against Saigon, Hue, Quang Tri, Da Nang, Nha Trang, Qui Nhon, Kontum, Ban Me Thuot, My Tho, Can Tho, and Ben Tre. They gained temporary control of ten provincial capitals, and in 13 of the towns and cities attacked, the communists made considerable inroads, but were generally expelled in two or three days. Only in Saigon and Hue was the fighting more protracted.

It is illuminating to look at three types of communist attack, namely those on the combat base at Bien Hoa, the logistics

General William C. Westmoreland visits the U.S. embassy after the end of the communist attack. It was a symptom of the acute breakdown in relations between the military and the media that the latter refused to accept the general's categorical assertion that there were no live attackers still inside the building.

Hue
For further references see pages 18, 20, 21, 107, 108, 109, 129

Da Nang
For further references see pages 13, 29, 51, 129

base at Tan Son Nhut, and the allied base area at Hue. Bien Hoa was attacked by two battalions and one reinforced infantry company, and for the loss of 30 U.S. Air Force personnel (four killed and 26 wounded), the allied forces killed 139 communists and captured another 25 on the base, while another 1,164 were killed and 98 captured in the general area; the USAF also lost two aircraft destroyed and another 20 damaged.

Tan Son Nhut was attacked by five battalions (one of sappers and four of infantry), and for the loss of 23 American (19 U.S. Army and four USAF) and 32 South Vietnamese personnel killed, and 86 American (75 U.S. Army and 11 USAF) and 79 South Vietnamese personnel wounded, the allied forces killed 962 communists and captured nine; the USAF also suffered damage to 13 aircraft.

The Battle for Hue

The longest fighting of the entire Tet offensive, was in Hue, an old imperial city of considerable historical and cultural importance to the South Vietnamese. The fighting lasted until February 25, but partly because of the allies' initial reluctance to use air power and artillery for fear of causing irreparable damage to the historic city.

The communist attack started on January 31, when the 800th, 802nd, and 806th Battalions of the North Vietnamese 6th Infantry Regiment, supported by the North Vietnamese 12th Combat Engineer Battalion, moved into that part of Hue northwest of the bend in the River Huong. The 804th Battalion of the North Vietnamese 4th Infantry Regiment advanced into the part of the city lying southeast of the bend, supported by six Viet Cong battalions. Within hours, the communists had occupied all of Hue with the exception of the citadel, where the South Vietnamese 3rd Infantry Division had its headquarters, and the compound that housed the advisory team located in the area by the Military Assistance Command, Vietnam. The battle eventually involved 11 South Vietnamese battalions as well as seven American battalions (four army and three marine corps), and by the

The bitterest fighting of the entire Tet offensive was concentrated in the city of Hue. Here a group of marines shelters behind a blasted wall.

Gunnery Sergeant F. A. Thomas of Company ''H,'' 2nd Battalion, 5th Marine Regiment, 1st Marine Division, appears to be signalling a turn as he sits in a toy car beside a bullet-scarred wall during a pause in his unit's attempt to halt and reverse the communist advance in Hue.

time the last communists had been killed or had faded from sight on February 25, the Americans had fired 52,000 rounds of field artillery ammunition (between 105- and 203-mm/4.13- and 8-inch caliber) and 7,670 rounds of naval ammunition (5- and 8-inch/127- and 203-mm caliber); tactical air power had also delivered 536 tons of air-dropped ordnance.

The cost of the battle was horrendous. At the purely military level, the Americans lost 119 killed and 961 wounded, while the South Vietnamese suffered 363 killed and 1,242 wounded; on the other side, the communists lost about 5,000 men killed in Hue itself, and 3,000 more in the surrounding area. But the worst losses were those of the civilians. It is believed that about 5,800 were killed in the fighting, although only about 2,800 were buried, and about 116,000 more lost their homes.

An Undoubted Communist Defeat...

Throughout South Vietnam, the first 14 days of the Tet offensive cost the communists 32,000 dead and 5,800 taken prisoner, just half the total committed to the operation. By any standards these losses were appalling; the Americans and South Vietnamese respectively suffered

1,000 and 2,800 killed during the same period. Only at Hue did the communists take and hold ground for any appreciable time, which probably explains why they did not commit any reserves they had earmarked. Throughout the offensive, the main weight of the defensive fighting was borne by the South Vietnamese regular and militia forces; both performed well despite the fact that most units were under strength because so many men were away on Tet leave. Nowhere in South Vietnam was there any sign of a popular uprising to support the communists. All in all, therefore, the Tet offensive was a total failure at the military level, and both the allies and the communists perceived it as such.

In overall terms, the Tet offensive cost the communists 45,000 troops killed and another 6,991 taken prisoner; the communists also lost about 1,300 crew-served weapons and 7,000 or more small arms. The allies lost 4,324 men killed, 16,063 men wounded, and 598 men missing. The civilian casualties of South Vietnam, which amounted to some 14,000 dead, 24,000 wounded, and perhaps 630,000 left homeless must be added to the total. With the civilian casualties left out, the communists had clearly lost the Tet offensive.

...Becomes a Major Success

Initially, the only people who saw the situation in another light were some of the American media teams in South Vietnam. One of these men, Peter Braestrup of the *Washington Post*, later wrote: ''Rarely has contemporary crisis-journalism turned out, in retrospect, to have veered so widely from reality.'' Without any notable exception, the American journalists forgot or ignored the warnings that had earlier been issued by Westmoreland and other U.S. officers, and claimed that the allies had been taken completely by surprise, had fought a disorganized campaign, and had only just avoided complete disaster! The

A military convoy edges its way down a street in Hue that had been heavily damaged in the fighting of the Tet offensive.

campaign was certainly disorganized, but this resulted from the way it had been planned by the communists. At no stage had the allies even approached disaster. As Charles B. MacDonald, an eminent historian of the period, has put it, none of the errant journalists "thought to draw parallels with other wars in which a losing side had staged a grand surprise assault – as Germany had in 1918 and in late 1944. Confirmed in their long-held skepticism, they were determined to expose the subterfuge and chicanery they saw behind the Johnson administration's claims of progress. There was no conspiracy among them, merely a group reaction based on shared biases and imperceptions..."

In the towns and cities affected by the fighting, the damage was fairly slight by the standards of World War II and the Korean War. But to the media, it was appalling, and television can sometimes mislead its viewers by suggestion that damage in one area is widespread. In addition, some American forces personnel were ill-prepared to deal with instant news reporting, made extremely damaging statements: in Ben Tre, for example,

about a quarter of the town was severely damaged, and an officer was quoted as saying that "it became necessary to destroy the town to save it."

The media saw the destruction not as a consequence of the communist offensive, but as a result of the air and artillery power used by the allies. They also focused on civilian casualties and refugees, but totally ignored the fact that, during their occupation of Hue and other cities, the communists had tortured or executed some 5,000 South Vietnamese. Rumor or supposition reported as fact tends to acquire a life of its own, and it proved very difficult to persuade the American public that the imperial palace in Hue had not been destroyed but only slightly damaged, and that Saigon was not a devastated city in which fires raged unchecked.

Another major target for the rumor and supposition machine was Khe Sanh. Here the media did just as the communists would have liked and in effect created a potential Dien Bien Phu. The media suggestion that the allies had elected to stand and fight at Khe Sanh ignored the vulnerability of the site. A refusal to

One of the most important tactical warplanes operated by the Americans over Vietnam was the Douglas A-4 Skyhawk, the so-called "bantam bomber." Designed for carrierborne operations, it was also extensively used from land bases. This is an A-4E of the U.S. Marine Corps' VMA-223 squadron.

His hands on the butt and trigger of his 0.5-inch (12.7-mm) caliber M2 heavy machine gun, the commander of an M113 vehicle of the 1st Platoon, 1st Squadron, 4th Cavalry Regiment, keeps his eyes open for any sign of communist movement during a sweep through the "Iron Triangle." Below the man is a row of colored smoke grenades.

defend the U.S. Marine Corps and South Vietnamese Ranger garrison at Khe Sanh would have condemned them to almost certain destruction. At this well-prepared and nicely sited fire-support base, 6,000 allied soldiers (one-sixtieth of the combat troops available to Westmoreland) were holding a North Vietnamese force of some 20,000 men. Estimates of the North Vietnamese strength against Khe Sanh throughout the siege range from a low of a few thousand to a high of 50,000. Whatever their actual strength, these troops were wasted and would have been far better employed in aiding the main part of the Tet offensive, a fact that was glibly ignored by the American media.

Interestingly enough, the negative media reports did affect the American public, but in the short term the effect of the unfavorable way the Tet offensive was reported rallied the American people to the administration. Only when President Johnson failed to retaliate strongly against the communists did an increasingly large proportion of the American public finally begin to turn against the administration's handling of the war.

Media Influence in Washington

Where the media did have a profound effect, though, was on members of Congress and on the middle ranks of the influential Washington bureaucratic machine. In Congress, "hawk" senators and representatives were abashed and fell comparatively silent, while their more "dovish" counterparts imagined a groundswell of support under them and became more vociferous. In the administration, many bureaucrats felt it difficult to reconcile the official reports crossing their desks with the striking images emerging from their television sets, and many people gradually accepted the more compelling visual imagery as reality.

Ho Chi Minh Trail
For further references see pages 25, 61, 79, 80, 82, 90, 104, 112

An M48 tank of the U.S. Marine Corps waits as marine engineers sweep the road for communist mines during the advance of the allied relief force headed for beleaguered Khe Sanh.

Westmoreland was confident in his assessment of the Tet offensive as a military defeat for the communists, but remained cautiously concerned that the defeat had not been heavy enough to prevent other offensives in the near future. General Earle G. Wheeler, chairman of the Joint Chiefs of Staff, saw in this a way not only to bolster American strength in South Vietnam, but also to rebuild the strength of the ground forces stationed in the United States where the strategic reserve at home had fallen to a single division. The recent North Korean seizure of the communications ship U.S.S. *Pueblo* was a possible herald of further tension in the Far East, and U.S. planners were also concerned about the possibility of renewed trouble in Berlin and in the Middle East. Wheeler therefore urged Westmoreland to request additional troops. Westmoreland requested a large reinforcement in the hope that they would give the Americans and their allies

a decisive edge in South Vietnam. It could also provide the means to develop a local reserve that could be used to invade Laos and/or Cambodia to sever the Ho Chi Minh and Sihanouk trails if such moves were ever permitted, or for an amphibious operation to trap North Vietnamese troops in the Demilitarized Zone. Wheeler and Westmoreland also hoped that, by calling reservists into federal service and heavily reinforcing the men available to Military Assistance Command, Vietnam, they could convince the communists that, despite opposition at home, the U.S. really meant business in South Vietnam.

President Johnson was very worried about the request for another 206,000 men, of which half were earmarked for the strategic reserve and half for South Vietnam. The president therefore ordered the matter to be considered by two bodies, one of them a committee chaired by Secretary of Defense Clark M. Clifford and

One of the weapons most favored by the Viet Cong was the portable rocket launcher, which was light yet packed an effective punch. The types most frequently used by the communists were the RPG-2 and later RPG-7, both of them Soviet weapons designed for use against armored vehicles, but also effective against a variety of other targets. The rocket fired by the RPG-7 is the PG-7 grenade, which is percussion-fired from the launcher. The fins unfold to stabilize the projectile as it leaves the launcher. After the projectile has traveled about 33 feet, its rocket motor fires to propel it a further 330 yards, where its warhead can penetrate about 12 inches of armor. The warhead used in this and comparable weapons is the hollow-charge type. Its method of operation is described in the accompanying diagrams, from left to right the warhead, the launch, the impact and fuse initiation, and the detonation. The warhead is comparatively wide because the amount of armor it can penetrate is directly proportional to the diameter of the explosive charge. Set into this charge, point inward, is a hollow cone of copper, and in front of this is the nose cone. Its impact detonator makes sure that the warhead detonates at the right stand-off distance from the armor to be penetrated. The design of the warhead means that detonation creates a forward-flowing plume of incandescent gas that vaporizes the copper cone and creates a metal/gas jet that concentrates to a focus point on the outer surface of the target armor. This phenomenally hot and fast-moving jet burns a hole in the armor and erupts into the vehicle's interior, spraying the inside with metal fragments and the residue of the metal/gas jet, which is still lethally hot.

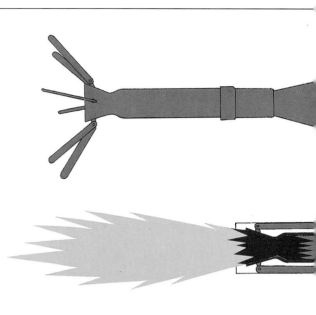

the other a panel composed of a number of respected ex-military men. Perhaps swayed by the media coverage of the Tet offensive, both bodies recommended against any reinforcement.

Johnson accepted the recommendation, but, before he could announce the fact, the *New York Times* informed the country that the administration was considering the despatch of another vast contingent of U.S. soldiers to South Vietnam. In a fashion that was now completely standard, the media reaction was wholly negative.

Westmoreland's correct assessment of the Tet offensive's outcome was confirmed by the poor performance of the communists in the following months. They did try two follow-up offensives (one in May and the other in August), but they were confined mainly to rocket and mortar attacks and achieved little more than nuisance value. The tactical and operational initiative thus passed to the allies. The flagging "rural pacification" program picked up momentum once again; allied control was soon resumed in areas that had been overrun by the communists and then expanded to new areas; and recruitment for the South Vietnamese services improved.

Abrams Succeeds Westmoreland

At this point, there was a major change in the U.S. command. President Johnson revealed the appointment of Westmoreland to the position of U.S. Army Chief of Staff and his succession as commander in South Vietnam by General Creighton W. Abrams. It is symptomatic of the breakdown of relations between the administration and the media that, although the decision had been made in January, well before the beginning of the Tet offensive, the announcement brought the claim that the president was unhappy with Westmoreland for his performance in the Tet offensive and had "kicked him upstairs" to make room for Abrams.

In an effort to placate media hostility, the president now yielded to pressure from the antiwar movement and the increasing "dove" mood of officials in his own administration. He

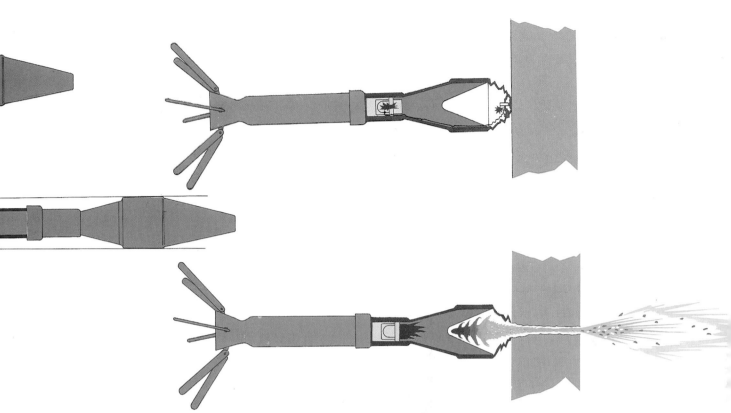

The Battle for Khe Sanh

ordered another bombing halt and again invited the communists to the conference table. In an effort to give greater credibility to his offer, Johnson also revealed that he would not be standing for reelection in the presidential elections scheduled for the fall of 1968. The antiwar movement immediately claimed that it had managed to hound Johnson from office.

Fruitless Talks

To the surprise of all, the North Vietnamese finally agreed to participate in talks. Yet the ray of hope offered by this positive response was soon clouded. When talks did start in Paris, it soon became clear that the North Vietnamese had no real intention of negotiating anything but trivial matters. Their real interest lay in pinning the Americans to the negotiating process and world opinion as the communists rebuilt their strength for a resurgence of their military effort in South Vietnam.

Throughout this period, the North Vietnamese had been continuing their effort against the fire support base at Khe Sanh. Lying 14 miles south of the Demilitarized Zone and a mere 6 miles east of the South Vietnamese border with Laos, the base's artillery and infantry posed a severe threat to the Ho Chi Minh Trail. As early as 1962, when the American presence in South Vietnam amounted to just 10,000 advisers, the importance of Khe Sanh had been recognized, and men of the U.S. Army Special Forces, the ''Green Berets,'' had established the beginnings of the base as a camp for long-range patrol units. The communists did not respond at first, but in January 1966 the base was shelled; and during the rest of the year, communist pressure on the base gradually increased.

The increasing threat to the base was soon appreciated by the Americans, and late in 1966 it was decided that Khe Sanh needed

Right: A Fairchild C-123 Provider light transport lands at Khe Sanh with supplies and reinforcements as the North Vietnamese open fire on the runway with mortars. The Provider landed safely and, after disgorging its load, took off without problems.

Opposite Top: The U.S. Marines had made effective use of the flamethrower as a close-range weapon in World War II and repeated this experience in the Vietnam War. This corporal at Khe Sanh is using his flamethrower around the fire base's perimeter.

Opposite Below: Chinese arms and ammunition were supplied to the communists. This ammunition store was found and destroyed by a unit of the 5th Cavalry.

Right: Other aircraft were not as fortunate as the Provider seen above. This is the wreckage of a Sikorsky CH-53 Sea Stallion heavy helicopter shot down at Khe Sanh.

a heavier defense than the Green Berets could provide. In January 1967, therefore, the Green Berets moved west to the Montagnard village of Lang Vei, and Khe Sanh was garrisoned by Colonel John Lanigan's 3rd Marine Regiment. With the base beginning to assume considerable importance, it was decided that an airstrip was essential, and a naval "Seabee" (construction battalion) unit created a 1,500-foot runway of pierced-steel planks. By the middle of May 1967, the 3rd Marine Regiment had cleared the communists off the adjacent hilltops and was replaced by Colonel John Padley's 26th Marine Regiment. The men of the new garrison immediately began the laborious task of improving the base's defenses. They were, however, severely hampered by shortages of heavy equipment and supplies as the runway deteriorated after a multitude of landings

by heavily laden Lockheed C-130 Hercules four-engined transports. Use of the lighter de Havilland Canada C-7 twin-engined transport eased matters, but this plane could not carry the panels of aluminum matting that were to replace the steel planks. Eventually, the air force used the parachute-extraction system to deliver the matting by C-130: as the plane passed over the airstrip at very low level, a parachute was streamed from the rear of the load to boom open immediately behind the plane and pull the load from the hold, whereupon it fell the few feet to the ground. The Seabees were thus able to rebuild the runway and lengthen it to 3,900 feet.

This made the delivery of supplies considerably easier, but the base was still no easy place to defend; for it was commanded by hills to the north and northwest, the River Quang Tri that supplied its drinking water ran through communist-controlled areas, and during the early months of the year, early-morning fog so reduced visibility that air operations and visual spotting were virtually impossible.

In December 1967, it became clear that the communists were massing considerable strength in the region around Khe Sanh in the form of the 20,000 or so men of the North Vietnamese 304th and 325th Infantry Divisions, with reinforcement available from the North Vietnamese 320th and 324th Infantry Divisions slightly farther to the rear. Patrols increasingly encountered heavy opposition, and in January 1968, a captured North Vietnamese officer admitted that the North Vietnamese were planning to overrun Khe Sanh and cut Route 9, the main west/east link between Laos and the South Vietnamese coast at Dong Ha.

The battle for Khe Sanh started on January 21, 1968, when the North Vietnamese launched an unsuccessful at-

One of the stalwarts of the U.S. Air Force in the Vietnam War was the McDonnell RF-101 Voodoo, the tactical reconnaissance version of the F-101 Voodoo interceptor fighter and fighter-bomber. The reconnaissance model had four low-altitude cameras in a lengthened nose and two high-altitude cameras behind the cockpit in place of the fighter version's cannon ammunition magazines. The RF-101's speed and stability at lower altitudes made it a first-class tactical reconnaissance platform, and it made its greatest contribution in the Vietnam War in this form. The main variant was the RF-101C, which was powered by two 14,880-pound (6,750-kg) afterburning thrust Pratt & Whitney J57-P-13 turbojets for a maximum speed of 1,012 miles per hour (1,629 km/h) or Mach 1·54 at 35,000 feet (10,670 m). The type had a maximum range of 2,145 miles (3,450 km) and could climb to an altitude of 55,300 feet (16,855 m). The RF-101C's dimensions included a span of 39 feet 8 inches (12·09 m) and a length of 69 feet 4 inches (21·13 m), and its empty and maximum take-off weights were 26,136 and 51,000 pounds (11,855 and 23,133 kg) respectively.

tack on a marine outpost on the eastern side of the River Quang Tri. As this effort faded away, the main base was attacked with artillery and mortars, whose projectiles tore great holes in the runway and set fire to the main dump with the loss of 1,340 tons of ammunition and one helicopter. The attack also killed 18 American troops and wounded 40. With the attack now firmly under way, the 3,500 marines pulled back into their carefully planned defensive positions, and all civilians were flown out to Da Nang.

In the North Vietnamese assault, the 325th Infantry Division moved forward on the base's northwestern side, occupying the dominating hills and establishing fire bases for the North Vietnamese artillery on Hills 881S and 861; other elements bypassed the marines' positions and cut Route 9. Slightly later, the 304th Division moved east on Lang Vei and the village of Khe Sanh, thereby completing the interception of Route 9 and approaching the fire support base at Khe Sanh from the southwest.

Khe Sanh Is Cut Off

Shortly after the beginning of the attack, the base at Khe Sanh had been cut off, and a large part of its vital ammunition destroyed. Brigadier General Burl McLaughlin, the U.S. Air Force officer in charge of aerial supply services, was advised that damage to the airstrip made it impossible for C-130s to land at Khe Sanh. He therefore ordered that an emergency air bridge be created with Fairchild C-123 Provider twin-engined transports, which flew in 116 tons of ammunition in slightly more than 24 hours.

Lieutenant General Robert E. Cushman, the commander of III Marine Amphibious Force, gave permission to Major General Rathvon C. Tompkins's 3rd

A machine gunner of Company "B," 1st Battalion, 16th Infantry Regiment, 1st Infantry Division, crosses a log bridge in the flat terrain typical of Gia Binh province.

A Sikorsky CH-54A Tarhe flying-crane army helicopter prepares to depart after flying in a bridge span used to repair a demolished bridge on Route 9. The exact point was about 4 ¼ miles from Khe Sanh.

Two radiomen of Company ''C,'' 1st Battalion, 7th Marine Regiment, 1st Marine Division, relay reports from forward units to headquarters during Operation ''Worth'' in March 1968.

Marine Division to reinforce the 26th Marine Regiment (now commanded by Colonel David Lownds) with the 1st Battalion of the 9th Marine Regiment. Lownds thus commanded five battalions (one of artillery and four of infantry) until January 26, when the marine were reinforced by the South Vietnamese 37th Ranger Battalion, increasing allied strength to about 6,000 men. With a large base to protect, Lownds decided that it was impossible to launch even a local counterattack to reopen Route 9. Thus Khe Sanh remained isolated, with air transport its sole source of supply.

The base was nonetheless a formidable obstacle for any communist movement, for its artillery strength included ten 106-mm (4·17-inch) recoilless rifles and the 90-mm (3·54-inch) guns of six M48 tanks. In addition, its regular establishment included 46 pieces of artillery in three light batteries with 105-mm (4·13-inch) howitzers, one medium battery with 155-mm (6·1-inch) howitzers, one battery with 4·2-inch (107-mm) mortars, and seven heavy batteries with eighteen 175-mm (6·89-in) long-range guns. The last were particularly important for cutting off communist forces. Before the battle's start, air force and navy aircraft had liberally seeded the area with acoustic and seismic sensors that relayed data to Nakhom Phanom in Thailand, where specialist teams determined the location, speed, and direction of communist convoys and radioed the information to the artillery at Khe Sanh. Within four days, other sensor fields were laid closer to Khe Sanh, allowing close-range interdiction of communist movements.

Limited North Vietnamese Success

During the first week in February, the North Vietnamese made several attacks on the base at Khe Sanh, but even when they managed to break through the barrages of artillery fire and deluges of air-dropped weapons, they ran into

Left: The Vietnam War was characterized by a major, but generally unsuccessful, psychological warfare campaign to win the ''hearts and minds'' of the South Vietnamese civilian population. Here a Douglas C-47 of the 6th Psychological Warfare Battalion drops propaganda leaflets over South Vietnam.

Below: Men of the 11th Marine Engineer Regiment swarm over a bridge as they rush preparations for Operation ''Pegasus,'' the allied effort to relieve the garrison of Khe Sanh.

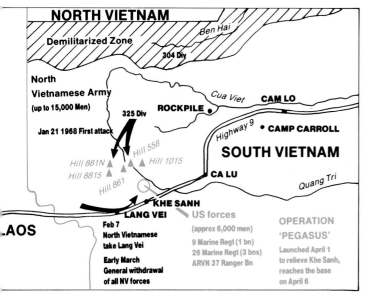

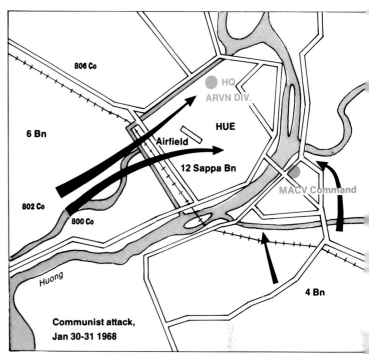

Above: The battle for Khe Sanh during the Tet Offensive.

Above Right: The recapture of Hue.

Above: Marines of the Khe Sanh garrison stand by the road running through the base as men of Company ''B,'' 5th Battalion, 7th Cavalry Regiment, 3rd Brigade, 1st Cavalry Division (Airmobile) pass through toward Hill 680 on April 8, 1968.

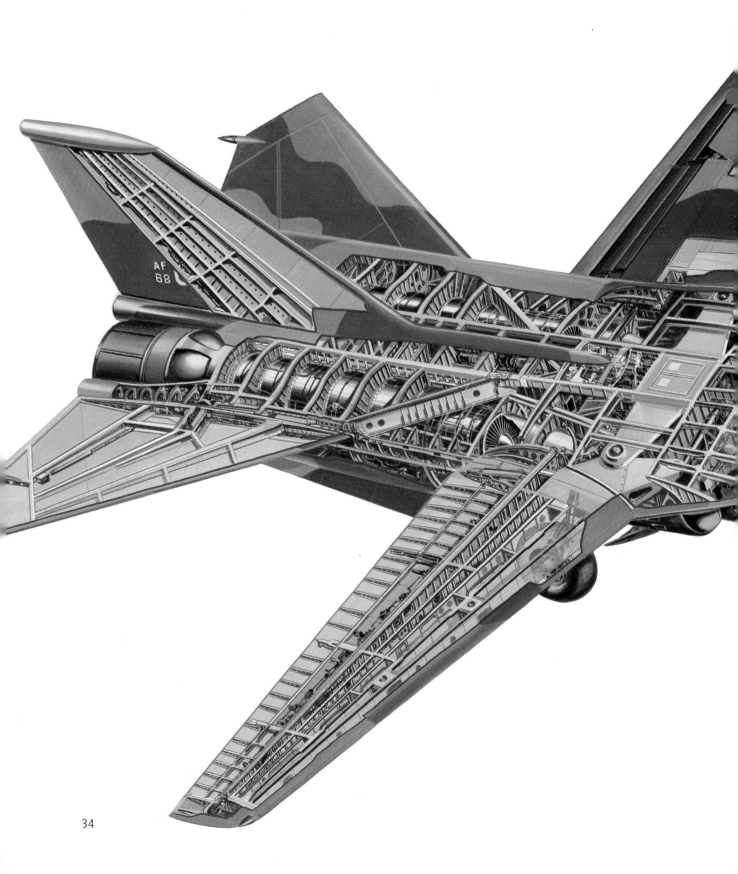

A warplane that made a disastrous debut in the Vietnam War, but then matured rapidly as a superb type, was the General Dynamics F-111, generally known as the "Aardvark." and the world's first operational variable-geometry warplane, in which the wings can be moved through a large angle between the minimum- and maximum-sweep positions. The 16° minimum-sweep position illustrated here provides maximum lift at low speeds resulting in a short take-off run with a heavy load. The intermediate-sweep positions provide a combination of long range at high subsonic cruising speed, and the 72·5° maximum-sweep position allows very high dash speed at high altitude or slightly supersonic speed without buffeting at very low level. The plane illustrated is an F-111E, not the F-111A that was generally used in the Vietnam War. It was powered by two 19,600-pound (8,891-kg) afterburning thrust Pratt & Whitney TF30-P-9 turbofans for maximum high- and low-altitude speeds of 1,450 and 800 miles per hour (2,335 and 1,287 km/h, Mach 2.2 and Mach 1.2) respectively. The empty and maximum take-off weights are 49,000 and 99,000 pounds (22,226 and 44,906 kg), the latter with the maximum 31,500-pound (14,290-kg) warload. Its dimensions include minimum- and maximum-sweep spans of 63 feet (19·20 m) and 31 feet 11½ inches (9·74 m). and a length of 73 feet 6 inches (22·40 m).

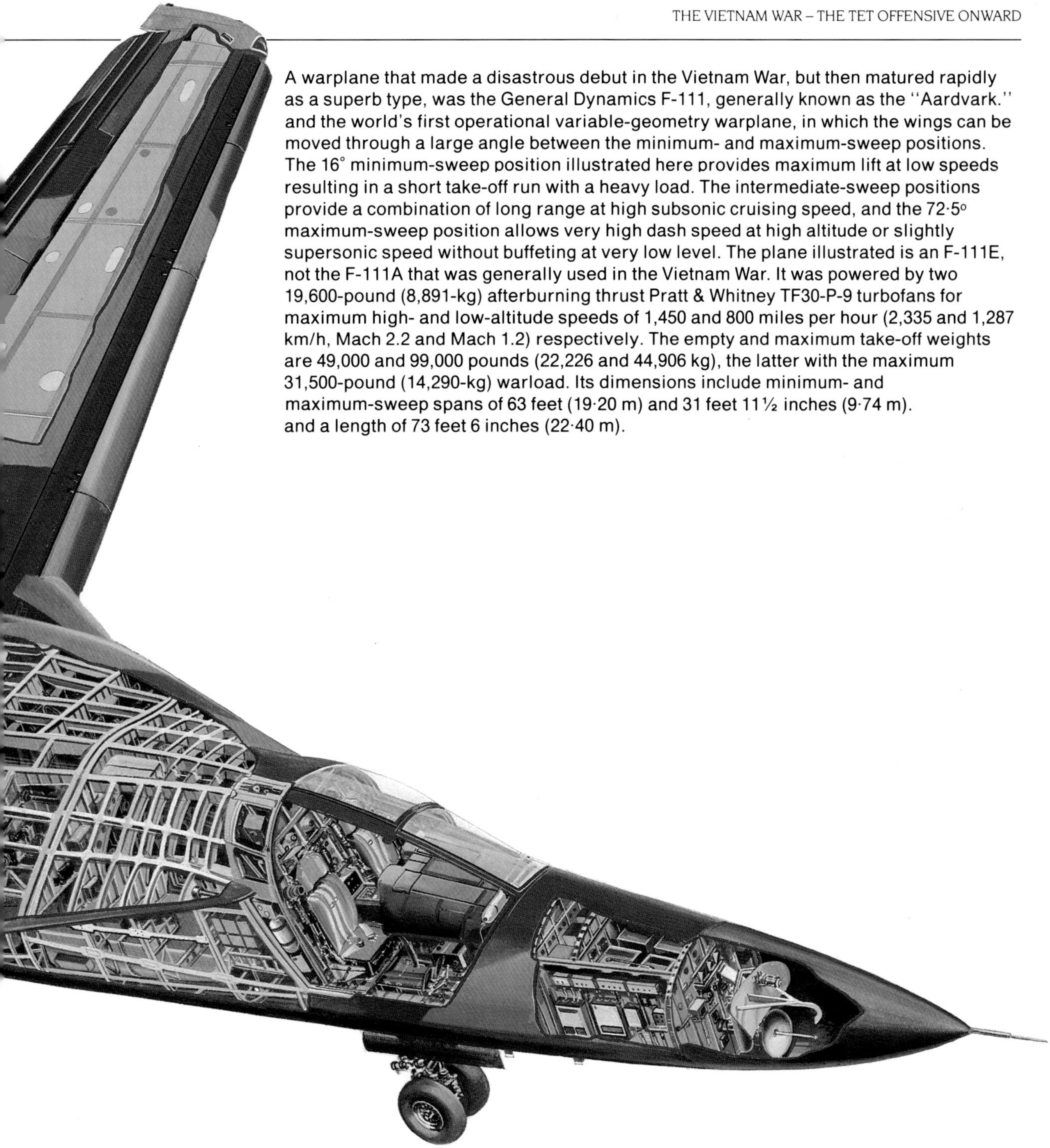

Part of the effort to defeat the communists at the psychological level was devoted to civic action such as medical and educational improvements for the South Vietnamese civil population. Here Sergeant Daniel G. Sherpherd, a medic of a Civic Action ''A'' Team, 5th Special Forces Group (Airborne), 1st Special Forces, applies ointment to the eyes of a Montagnard woman of Dak-Sak village.

determined marine resistance and could not reach the camp's main defenses. On February 8, the focus of attention shifted to Lang Vei, which was held by 24 Green Berets and 900 Montagnard irregulars plus some Laotian troops who had arrived a few days earlier after failing to check a communist thrust in their own country. A major North Vietnamese attack, supported by PT-76 light tanks, overran most of the camp despite heavy attacks by American tactical aircraft. Captain Frank C. Willoughby, the commander, called for reinforcement, but the North Vietnamese had occupied both of Lang Vei's helicopter landing zones and any overland advance from Khe Sanh would certainly be ambushed in the dark. Willoughby and some of the survivors

managed to escape; 14 Green Berets and 60 Montagnards reached Khe Sanh.

By February 11, the North Vietnamese had sited antiaircraft guns on the lines of approach to Khe Sanh, making air supply increasingly difficult. Despite liberal use of napalm – 53,600 tons were dropped around Khe Sanh in a 28-day period ending in mid-February – the North Vietnamese managed to continue their slow forward progress with infantry and artillery, and the first Hercules transport, carrying helicopter fuel, was lost to antiaircraft fire on February 11. This KC130 of the U.S. Marine Corps, carrying helicopter fuel, leaking fuel from punctured tanks, managed to touch down at Khe Sanh before bursting into flame and careering off the runway. The air effort into and around Khe Sanh was huge; it

The South Vietnamese forces also made a considerable though sporadic psychological warfare effort. Here a member of the 403rd Political Warfare Company, 7th Infantry Division, Army of the Republic of Vietnam, uses a loudspeaker to tell the villagers of Ap Trung about how they can help in the effort to keep Route 4 open in the region of My Tho.

has been estimated that the Khe Sanh region became the most heavily bombed area in the history of air warfare.

The North Vietnamese continued their attacks on the allied garrison, commanded in the later stages of the battle by Colonel Bruce Meyers, but failed to make significant inroads. Planning had begun on January 25 for a relief operation, only four days after the start of the battle, but the more urgent demands of meeting the Tet offensive forced a postponement. Thus it was only on April 1 that Operation ''Pegasus'' began with an advance by Major General John J. Tolson's 1st Cavalry Division (Airmobile) supported by a South Vietnamese airborne battalion. The South Vietnamese were the first to link up with the marines in Khe Sanh on April 6, and two days later, the 1st Cavalry

Division (Airmobile) also reached the marines' forward positions. Route 9 was clear by April 12 as the North Vietnamese faded away to the west and north, and the battle ended on April 14.

Khe Sanh: Worthwhile or Not?

The poor resistance to ''Pegasus'' suggests that by this time the North Vietnamese were no longer interested in capturing Khe Sanh, since the Tet offensive had ended in failure. It has also been suggested that the attack on Khe Sanh was a communist effort designed to tie down high-grade forces, especially air units, in the northwestern corner of South Vietnam at a time when they could have been better employed fighting the main

parts of the Tet offensive. Whatever the reasoning of the North Vietnamese, they were effectively held and beaten at Khe Sanh. Because they were able to pull back in good order, it is virtually impossible to ascertain their personnel losses. Proven materiel losses amounted to two antiaircraft guns, 207 crew-served weapons, 557 small arms, and 17 vehicles, including some PT-76 light tanks.

The North Vietnamese forces were supported by an unknown number of 152- and 130-mm (6- and 5·12-inch) pieces of artillery during the battle, firing a daily average of 150 rounds rising to a peak of 1,307 rounds on February 23. The allies had considerably greater artillery strength, as noted above, and fired a daily average of 2,065 rounds for an overall total of 158,981 rounds.

This huge quantity of ordnance was complemented by the efforts of the air forces, which dropped 1,607 tons of weapons in a daily average of 300 or more tactical warplane and 45 Boeing B-52 Stratofortress heavy bomber sorties. During the main 70-day period of the battle for Khe Sanh, more than 24,000 tactical and 2,700 heavy bomber sorties were flown to drop 98,215 tons of ordnance.

This was only part of the air effort, however, for tactical transport was absolutely vital to the continued existence of the base. Up to April 8, deliveries amounted to 11,071 tons, achieved in 601 parachute drops (496 by C-130s and 105 by C-123s), 57 parachute extractions from C-130s, and 460 landings (273 by C-130s, 179 by C-123s, and eight by C-7s). Air losses amounted to six fixed-wing aircraft (including three C-123s) and 17 marine helicopters, and another 35 marine helicopters were damaged.

The Origins of "Vietnamization"

In the aftermath of the Tet offensive and the successful defense of Khe Sanh,

With the ports of its two starboard-side 20-mm caliber cannon showing evidence of extensive use, this Vought F-8 Crusader of the 1st Marine Air Wing stands on the flight line ready for action. The underwing hardpoint carries tandem pairs of ''iron'' bombs, and the lateral hardpoint behind the cockpit carries two 5-inch (127-mm) caliber rockets. Note the raised leading edge of the wing, a feature designed to produce high lift at low speed, which shortens the take-off run. This fighter is designed for use on carriers.

the U.S. administration went through a period of intense soul-searching. It had been a tenet of the Kennedy and Johnson administrations that the war in South Vietnam was a conflict that only the South Vietnamese could win. Yet there had been an enormous growth in the number of American troops committed, and since 1965 South Vietnamese forces had played only a subsidiary role in operations. The main rationale was that the South Vietnamese forces' light equipment suited them to small-scale operations against the Viet Cong rather than large-scale operations against the better equipped North Vietnamese regulars.

In 1967, Washington's decision to restrict the number of U.S. forces committed in South Vietnam forced Westmoreland to reconsider this basic division of operational responsibilities and give the South Vietnamese a greater share. This tendency increased during 1968 as the United States began to anticipate an eventual withdrawal of American and North Vietnamese forces, leaving the South Vietnamese to deal with the Viet Cong In the aftermath of the Tet offensive, therefore, the U.S. launched a number of programs designed to increase

Left: Richard M. Nixon, the 39th president of the United States, was the prime architect of the American withdrawal from South Vietnam.

both the size and the fighting capability of the South Vietnamese forces. However, by the end of 1968, there had been no basic change in mission allocation: the Americans fought the North Vietnamese and the South Vietnamese handled the Viet Cong.

The basic policy altered after the in-

Below: Two Rome plows and a support vehicle based on the chassis of the M113 armored personnel carrier clear trees and brush of the type favored by the Viet Cong as protective cover. The men and equipment belonged to Company "D," 1st Engineer Battalion, 1st Infantry Division, operating in the Lai Khe area in June 1968.

auguration of President Richard M. Nixon in January 1969. The philosophy of the new administration was that the United States would provide weapons and logistical support for allied nations facing an insurgency problem, but that no U.S. ground forces should be committed. In April, Secretary of Defense Melvin R. Laird ordered the Pentagon to begin planning the withdrawal of U.S. forces from South Vietnam. In June, Nixon and Thieu met on Midway Island, and the United States announced the immediate removal of 25,000 men from South Vietnam. In September and December of the same year, similar announcements signaled the withdrawal of 35,000 and 50,000 more men respectively. These and later withdrawals were not planned to any far-sighted scheme, but implemented on a "where and when possible" basis stemming directly from the mood of American public opinion, the level of communist activity in South Vietnam, and the apparent capability of the South Vietnamese forces to deal with this activity. By the end

of 1969, though, it was clear that the United States was actively seeking to end its commitment in South Vietnam.

Despite the antiwar mood of the American public, for diplomatic reasons, this withdrawal would be possible only if the South Vietnamese were given an increased capacity to shoulder their own burden. Between 1965 and 1968, the strength of the South Vietnamese army rose from 250,000 to 427,000 men, and that of the Regional Force and the Popular Force from 264,000 to 393,000 men. The original South Vietnamese division of the country into four tactical zones, each accommodating a single corps, was retained, together with the ten established infantry divisions, each containing three four-battalion regiments.

The South Vietnamese Are Steadily Upgraded

The South Vietnamese army was thus expanded in its support elements. At the

An M60 machine gunner of the 1st Infantry Division wades through a muddy stream, typical of those in South Vietnam, during a search-and-destroy mission north of Phu Loi. In the course of this mission, a small Viet Cong base was discovered.

Richard M. Nixon
For further references see pages
39, 75, 81, 92, 93, 94, 97, 101, 102, 103, 125, 126, 127, 129

divisional level, the mortar battalion was replaced by two battalions of 105-mm (4.13-inch) field howitzers, and an armored cavalry squadron of light tanks and armored personnel carriers was added. At the same time, the engineer, signal, logistic, and other combat support elements were increased in size and capability. At the corps level, these headquarters were allocated several battalions of 155-mm (6.1-inch) howitzers, 20 battalions of Rangers, engineer and signal groups, and special logistic organizations containing ordnance, quartermaster, transportation, and depot units. At the highest level, the Joint General Staff headquarters controlled a reserve element of airborne and marine forces elevated from brigade to divisional level.

The militia forces were controlled by the 44 provinces and their subordinate districts, and were divided into the Regional Force and the Popular Force. The Regional Force included rifle companies, and the Popular Force was made up of rifle platoons. The South Vietnamese tried to amalgamate these lightly equipped forces into larger units, but their American advisers successfully argued that this would sacrifice the local nature and mobility of these units, which were well suited to preventing Viet Cong infiltration.

After the Tet offensive, South Vietnam decided on general mobilization, which coincided with the U.S. decision to make a major contribution to modernizing the South Vietnamese effort. Up to this time, the South Vietnamese had relied mainly on equipment inherited from the French or supplied by the U.S. from mothballed stocks: much of this equipment was adequate from the tactical point of view, but many items were worn out from long use. The first stage of the American contribution was the replacement of weapons of World War II vintage with modern items such as the M16 assault rifle, the M60 machine gun, and the M79 40-mm grenade launcher. Later stages of the program saw the

Marines of the 1st Platoon, Company "C," 1st Battalion, 9th Marine Regiment, 3rd Marine Division, take what cover they can during a communist mortar attack.

Opposite Top Left: Men of Company "B," 2nd Battalion, 7trh Cavalry Regiment, 1st Infantry Regiment, collect the inhabitants of a hamlet near Camp "Evans" for relocation to a protected village.

Opposite Top Right: A M60 machine gunner watches for any signs of communist activity on the bank of the My Cong River as a LCMB (Landing Craft Medium Mk 8) used by the commanding officer of the 1097th Transportation Company, 9th S&T Battalion, supports an operation by the 2nd Brigade of the 9th Infantry Division in July 1968.

Opposite Bottom: Marines of the 3rd Platoon, Company "M," 3rd Battalion, 7th Marine Regiment, 1st Marine Division, manage to keep their feet dry as they cross a paddy field in their operational area.

Right: A lance corporal of Company "E," 2nd Battalion, 3rd Marine Regiment, 3rd Marine Division, pauses for a drink of water during an operation in the hot and humid northern region of South Vietnam.

Below: A U.S. Navy patrol air-cushion vehicle, or hovercraft, glides smoothly but noisily over the still water of Cau Hai Bay near Hue.

introduction of modern radio equipment, vehicles, and other mechanical items.

The modernization programs of 1968 and 1969 had an effect on both troop strength and organization. Although the number of core rifle units (infantry, ranger, airborne, and marine) remained unaltered within the South Vietnamese establishment, the support and territorial units were substantially augmented, as noted above. This factor was directly inspired by the Americans, who rightly perceived that the basic "tooth" elements of the South Vietnamese forces were adequate for their tasks, but were let down by inadequate support units and the all-important "tail" elements, without which no first-line fighting unit can survive in the field.

An Offensive Role for the South Vietnamese Army

The object of the policy known as "Vietnamization" was twofold. In the first place, the planners hoped that the expanded and more capable units of the Regional Force and the Popular Force would be able to assume some of the local defense responsibilities of regular army battalions, thereby freeing these units for offensive operations. Thus the militia forces were steadily expanded and upgraded, and by 1972, they had a strength of more than 500,000 personnel. Over the same period and with a similar rationale in mind, the strength of the National Police was also increased. By 1972, the central government in Saigon could call on 116,000 members of the National Police and 550,000 territorial troops in 1,679 Regional Force companies and 8,356 Popular Force platoons.

In the second place, it was anticipated that the improvement of the South Vietnamese army's support forces would improve the combat capability and battlefield endurance of the first-line rifle forces. With this in mind, the United States provided financing and equipment that allowed the armored cavalry

The Vietnam War was characterized by the supply of vast quantities of American equipment to allied nations. Here a sergeant of the Royal Thai army uses masking tape to make a stencil for marking the Thai insignia and number on the boom of a newly delivered Bell UH-1H helicopter.

Private, Infantry, U.S. Army, Vietnam, 1967

This infantry private is typical of the American soldier in South Vietnam during 1969. He wears the pants of the cotton jungle utility uniform that appeared late in 1965 together with the later style of jungle boot, a cotton T shirt, and a floppy bush or "Jones" hat. The soldier carries the standard 5.56-mm (0.22-inch) caliber M16A1 assault role, and the rest of his lightweight equipment consists of extra ammunition magazines, a backpack on a frame with extra water bottles, and M18 smoke grenades.

45

squadrons to be increased in number from 10 to 20, permitted the establishment of four artillery battalions for each division and others for control at corps level, and made possible the creation of 18 aviation companies with more than 500 helicopters. The resulting improvement in the support forces has already been mentioned, including moves that affected engineer, signal, ordnance, military police, transport, medical, naval, and air elements.

More Modern Weapons

In 1970, Secretary of Defense Laird authorized the Consolidated Improvement and Modernization Program, which almost inevitably received the acronymic nickname "Crimp," an attempt to create an establishment for the South Vietnamese forces after the departure of the U.S. forces. Crimp foresaw further increases in the strength of the support elements and territorial forces, and also made provision for the use of civil contractors in technical matters such as long-range communica-

tions and the maintenance of high-technology weapons, both beyond South Vietnamese capabilities. Crimp was constantly adapted and modernized in line with operational requirements and anticipated communist responses, and eventually was allocated equipment such as antiaircraft weapons, antitank missiles, M48 battle tanks, and 175-mm (6·89-inch) self-propelled guns were allocated to the South Vietnamese forces.

Like early efforts to modernize the South Vietnamese forces, the many forms of the definitive Crimp were built on several assumptions. The first was the retention in South Vietnam of a major "residual support force" or, in the event that the North Vietnamese withdrew their forces, a large body of advisers. The second was continued U.S. logistic support of South Vietnam in supplies, equipment munitions, and, in the case of high-technology systems, maintenance. The third was a protracted American contribution to the fighting through the use of air power at all levels from tactical support to strategic bombing.

In overall terms, therefore, the policy of "Vietnamization" envisaged that all the

These river monitors are tied alongside a tug after being unloaded from the dock landing ship U.S.S. *Carter Hall* in Vung Tau harbor on the South Vietnamese coast of the South China Sea in August 1968. The bar armor provided protection against the kind of antitank weapons much favored by the communists; it detonated the warhead some distance away from any vulnerable spot. This means that the warhead's jet of hot gas and molten metal dissipated in the air instead of burning through the metal.

ground fighting would be undertaken by South Vietnamese forces, organized at three levels. At the lowest level, territorial and police units were to provide local security. At the middle level, the Civilian Irregular Defense Groups (the Montagnard border protection force created by the U.S. Army Special Forces) would use specially created ranger battalions, reinforced by organic 105-mm (4.13-inch) howitzer platoons, to detect and slow any North Vietnamese movements across the border into South Vietnam. At the highest level, the regular forces would deal with any problems in jungle and/or western border areas.

Everyone concerned with the "Vietnamization" program realized that the South Vietnamese lacked the air-mobility capability that was giving the American forces such tactical flexibility, but thought that the network of strategic roads constructed over the previous five years would provide adequate capability for rapid response anywhere in the country that a threat evolved. This network of high-speed paved roads had been produced by U.S. and South Vietnamese army engineers in conjunction with civil

contractors, and its maintenance was one reason for the expansion of the South Vietnamese army's engineer corps.

Niggling Doubts Begin to Surface

It all looked good and fine on paper and sounded even better in the mouths of its protagonists. But even from its beginning, many American commanders doubted the program. In a survey undertaken in February 1969, many American commanders with local experience expressed reservations about the long-term viability of "Vietnamization": virtually all agreed that the revived South Vietnamese army would be able to deal with the Viet Cong threat, but almost all agreed that it would not be capable of handling a major invasion by North Vietnamese forces.

The doubters based their fears not on the basic organization and equipment of the South Vietnamese forces, but on the very nature of South Vietnam's intertwined political and military systems. At the political level, there was a manifest reluctance to tackle the overall situation. There was no planning for longer-term

A marine sergeant of the 4th Platoon, Company "B," mans his 0·5-inch (12·7-mm) heavy machine gun to provide line-of-march security for the 1st Marine Division's 1st Tank Battalion.

Opposite: U.S. Navy warships operating in the South China Sea off the coast of South Vietnam could provide the forces on shore with heavy and accurate gunfire support. Here the battleship U.S.S. *New Jersey* lets fly with one of the 16-inch (406-mm) guns of her three triple turrets.

Right: This U.S. Navy PCF (Patrol Craft Fast) is seen off the South Vietnamese coast near An Thpoi. This type was used to intercept civilian craft that might be trying to run soldiers and equipment into the country.

Below: This aerial photograph of Fire Support Base "Cates," located southeast of the "Vandegrift" Combat Base in the 3rd Marine Division's operational area, provides a clear view of a typical fire-support base.

Men of the 4th Marine Regiment, 3rd Marine Division, move down a river in the Demilitarized Zone while searching for North Vietnamese positions, personnel, and supplies.

realities, only for shorter-term expediencies. In addition, there was enormous corruption, and there was a general lack of confidence and low morale that spread into the population at large. At the military level, there was an interlinked problem of low morale, poor pay, a system of officer appointments based on graft and influence, and a promotion ladder that favored the urban middle class over the rural lower class. Combined with these factors was a lack of high-ranking officers with genuine planning and command experience: when American forces had arrived, South Vietnamese officers had been relegated to subordinate functions in the planning and control of operations.

American Skills "Rubbing Off" onto the South Vietnamese?

Abrams was particularly concerned to improve the combat capabilities of South Vietnamese units. He arranged a large-scale program in which American forces were "paired" with comparable South Vietnamese forces in the hope that the skills of the Americans might spread by some intangible process to the South Vietnamese. Another reason for the program was that as the

American formations departed from the country, they would leave in place South Vietnamese formations already acquainted with the geography and operational requirements of the areas for which they would be responsible. The program did yield some useful results, but experience showed that South Vietnamese formations tended to revert to an apathetic state when their U.S. partners departed, either temporarily on a special task or permanently to the United States. The sole exception was the Hue-based South Vietnamese 1st Infantry Division under the command of Major General Ngoc Quang Truong, perhaps the ablest field commander in the South Vietnamese army.

One major objective of "Vietnamization" was a greater combat role for South Vietnamese formations and therefore a reduction in American casualties. This, it was hoped in Washington, would help to make the continued but smaller U.S. commitment to the war more palatable to the American public. Fewer American losses, the administration believed, would mean less antiwar feeling and, as a result, greater flexibility for the military in matters such as the bombing campaign, the expansion of the "Vietnamization" policy, a slower rate of

Creighton W. Abrams
For further references see pages
24, 81, 86, 90

withdrawal for U.S. forces, and greater freedom to intervene in Laos and perhaps even Cambodia.

Dashed Hopes for the Nixon Administration

The administration's hopes of making the Vietnam War more acceptable to the American people seemed well on the way to realization until the public revelation of two events in 1969: the My Lai massacre in April and the Battle of "Hamburger Hill" in May.

The first to hit the headlines was "Hamburger Hill," a single episode in a campaign that had become increasingly wearisome to the American leadership in South Vietnam. The Tet offensive and the siege of Khe Sanh had brought home to the communists the devastating effect of U.S. firepower, which had resulted in a gradual alteration in the nature of the communist ground war. Worried by the casualties that could be inflicted by American weapons and anticipating that the U.S. would soon pull out of the ground war, the communists decided to avoid head-on confrontations. Instead, they saved their strength and sought to keep the allies off balance with hit-and-run operations. As a result, most North Vietnamese and Viet Cong units retired over the South Vietnamese border into Cambodia and Laos, leaving in South Vietnam only a small number of units that

were divided into parties of between ten and 30 men based in strongholds in jungle areas.

During 1969, the communists achieved considerable success in three operations. They were small, but they nonetheless helped to remind the world that the communists were still a force to be feared. Typical of these operations was that of August 11, when carefully coordinated Viet Cong forces simultaneously attacked 179 scattered allied bases with artillery, mainly rockets and mortar bombs, and then followed up with infantry attacks. The damage caused and the casualties inflicted were small, but the operation served to confirm that the Viet Cong were still in action, and that the command structure was still capable of planning and implementing large-scale operations should it be thought desirable.

In an effort to detect and pin Viet Cong units, the allied forces could use basically the same tactic, splitting battalions into small units that undertook a large but undefined campaign of patrols, ambushes, and small-scale skirmishes in areas thought to contain Viet Cong bases, such as the Michelin rubber plantation north of Saigon, the coast of Quang Nam province south of Da Nang, and the A Shau valley on South Vietnam's northern border with Laos.

It was in this last area that the costly but fruitless Battle of "Hamburger Hill" started on May 14.

This Fairchild AC-119 of the U.S. Air Force's 71st Special Operations Squadron, seen here in flight near Nha Trang Air Base, was a potent gunship. Its weapons were arranged to fire sideways and at a downward angle to saturate the target area as the gunship orbited above it.

Men of the 101st Airborne Division, supported by South Vietnamese forces, encountered strong communist forces on Hill 937, otherwise known as Ap Bia Mountain and later "Hamburger Hill," about one mile inside the South Vietnamese frontier with Laos. The first allied attacks were repulsed by Viet Cong infantry in well-sited defensive positions, and the battle became one of attrition between the two opposing bodies of infantry. The allied forces launched nine assaults in six days, and both sides suffered very heavy losses before the allies took the hill. As the allied success became imminent, the communists fell back into the sanctuary offered by Laos, so the allied victory was empty, and it was followed a few days later by a withdrawal from this now-pointless objective.

A Wasted Effort

The battle had taken place only because the Viet Cong had elected to stand and fight under geographical conditions that suited them. As soon as the Americans committed substantial forces to the battle and gained the upper hand, the Viet Cong melted away. In overall terms, the battle was a waste of effort and lives. Once the Viet Cong had chosen to stand, it would probably have been better to call in the B-52 Stratofortress heavy bombers, which could have used their radar bombing systems to carpet the entire area with high-explosive bombs and thereby inflict heavy losses on the Viet Cong as they awaited an infantry attack.

The Battle of "Hamburger Hill" was one of the few large-scale operations of 1969 and therefore attracted considerable media attention. Reports of the battle were therefore extensive and served to infuriate the American public. Still more than before, the general sentiment was that the U.S. military machine in South Vietnam was led by incompetent commanders who committed their men to battles that served no military purpose.

The following November, the American public first became aware of the My Lai massacre, which had taken place on

The Lockheed C-130 Hercules, the air transport workhorse of the Vietnam War, was operated in a number of forms for specialist tasks. This is an HC-130 used as a flying command post for operations to locate and rescue downed aircrew. The folded-back probes on the nose could be swept forward to create a fork that could be used to recover parachute-fitted items from the air. They were then hooked and pulled through the rear doors into the cargo hold.

March 16, 1968. In April 1969, a Vietnam veteran wrote several open letters to the president and other prominent figures about rumors of a massacre perpetrated by Company "C," 1st Battalion, 20th Infantry Regiment, 23rd Infantry Division (Americal), during the previous year. In September, the army began a formal investigation of the matter and in due course Lieutenant William L. Calley, Jr., was charged with the murder of 100 or more South Vietnamese civilians. The matter was still largely unknown to the general public until November, when a series of media reports began to unfold the real horror of the event.

The My Lai Massacre

It eventually became clear that on March 16, 1968, the company of soldiers in question had landed by helicopter near My Lai, a village in the "free-fire zone" around Quang Ngai, a provincial capital. Under an indifferent commander, the inexperienced soldiers had begun to suffer casualties from snipers and booby traps, and quickly lost all sense of proper discipline. Calley extemporized a sweep into My Lai, but instead of encountering the anticipated communist troops, the soldiers found only old men, women, and children. In one of the most dishonorable episodes involving U.S. service personnel, the village was systematically destroyed over the next few hours. No fewer than 347 innocent civilians were murdered.

After these public revelations, the army established a mixed military and civilian investigatory panel under Lieutenant General William Peers to consider why 1968 inquiries had not revealed the massacre. After extensive work between

Cautious marines keep their guns trained on the entrance to a communist bunker after sending in a North Vietnamese prisoner to recover the bodies of his dead comrades.

November 1969 and March 1970, when more than 400 people were interviewed, the panel recommended that charges be brought against 15 officers, including Major General Samuel Koster, the former divisional commander who was then commandant of the U.S. Military Academy at West Point. The results of the panel's investigations stunned the American military and people alike. Here was official confirmation of what many had discounted as scurrilous journalism at its worst. It was more disturbing still to many Americans that the charges against senior officers were later dismissed before the matter came to court-martial, suggesting that there was one rule for senior officers and another for their subordinates. Calley was eventually sentenced to life imprisonment, reduced by a review board to 20 years, and finally shortened to a token sentence before he was released and dishonorably discharged in 1974.

The revelations of the investigatory panel regarding the My Lai massacre were shocking enough. Just as worrying, however, were the other conclusions: the massacre was not a single episode

(indeed, another massacre on the same day is thought to have resulted in the deaths of 50 civilians in a nearby village); most of the field-grade officers of the Americal Division had little or no knowledge of what was happening in the field; and the military had a tendency to play down negative factors while exaggerating positive ones without offering any real effort at confirmation.

Thus, the official report of the My Lai action, the American public now learned, had reported the killing of 128 Viet Cong and the capture of three weapons. That such a tendency could conceal an episode such as the My Lai massacre also threw into question the validity of "body count" thinking. Often, junior officers had reported the killing of many enemy soldiers but the capture of very few weapons. It now became abundantly clear that these reports were made to satisfy more senior battalion- and regimental-level officers, who passed on the information to their divisional and corps commanders without query, thereby guaranteeing that these career officers gained the credit for successful operations. In operations as fluid and

McDonnell Douglas F-4 Phantom II multirole fighters of the U.S. Marines' VFMA-232 squadron refuel from Lockheed KC-130F tankers during a deployment flight across the Pacific Ocean.

ill-defined as those in South Vietnam, body and weapon counts were the only real measure of the success of allied fighting units. So the complete assessment of the war to date was called into dispute by the inevitable questioning of the body count's validity in the aftermath of the My Lai massacre: had American and allied forces really killed the numbers of Viet Cong and North Vietnamese they claimed, especially when the weapon count was often considerably smaller than the body count?

A Revitalized South Vietnamese Defense

In this and other respects, 1969 was not a good period for the American forces in Vietnam, but in December there was some cause for optimism. President Thieu had consolidated South Vietnamese political power by replacing the civilian prime minister, Tran Van Huong, by an experienced soldier, General Tran Thien Khiem, and had revitalized the defense of the Saigon area by recalling a highly respected soldier, General Do Cao

Tri, and putting him in command of the three divisions located around the South Vietnamese capital. The policy of ''Vietnamization'' was moving ahead and, the Americans thought, was beginning to yield results. The pace of the war was definitely slowing; during the last months of the year, combat had declined to its lowest level since 1964. This suggested to the Americans that the communists were beginning to tire of the struggle, which according to allied estimates had cost them 132,000 dead in the previous 12 months.

American losses over the same period had been 9,249 killed, 69,043 wounded, and 112 missing. Even though the validity of the body count had been called into question, there could be little doubt that communist losses exceeded those of the allies by a very considerable margin. The U.S. administration could logically hope that the North Vietnamese might be more prepared to start meaningful discussions at the Paris negotiations.

Yet the North Vietnamese also had reason for satisfaction, despite the death of Ho Chi Minh during September. They had infiltrated into South Vietnam a large

U.S. Navy PBRs (Patrol Boat Rover) move along one of South Vietnam's many rivers during a routine sweep to intercept communist movements.

Do Cao Tri
For further references see pages 65, 66, 68, 78

Above: Marines of the Recoilless Rifle Platoon, Headquarters and Service Company, 2nd Battalion, 5th Marine Regiment, 1st Marine Division, have a height advantage in their position on Hill 483, 8 miles southeast of An Hoa Combat Base. They fire their 106-mm (4·17-inch) caliber weapon on communist positions on Que Son Mountain during Operation ''Durham Peak'' in August 1969.

Right: A scout/sniper ''scopes out'' a hillside near a position occupied by men of Company ''C,'' 1st Battalion, 3rd Marine Regiment, 3rd Marine Division.

Men of the 1st Marine Division's 1st Reconnaissance Battalion demonstrate the special extraction procedure used with the Boeing Vertol CH-46 Sea Knight helicopter in areas of South Vietnam where thick jungle canopy prevented more orthodox methods from being used.

number of soldiers (estimated by allied intelligence at 115,000) and could therefore maintain in the south a strength of about 250,000 men: 100,000 North Vietnamese soldiers, 50,000 Viet Cong main force troops, and 100,000 Viet Cong regional force soldiers and militia. Most of the larger and more capable formations were stationed just over the border in Cambodia and Laos, waiting for the moment that American strength in South Vietnam fell to a very low level. Life was therefore more than usually dangerous for the smaller and less capable communist forces inside South Vietnam. These "local" units had suffered such

high losses during the Tet offensive that they were now largely composed of troops born in South Vietnam.

Limited Operations in 1970

The tendencies evident in 1969 continued through 1970; the war was still one of small-scale actions. The communists favored rocket and mortar attacks on the allies' fixed installations such as fire support bases, airfields, and supply dumps, while the allies showed a preference for extensive patrols by small units with the intention of locating and ambushing

Although it carried a smaller payload than the Lockheed C-130 Hercules, the de Havilland Canada C-7A had an advantage. Its excellent STOL (Short Take-Off and Landing) performance allowed it to get into and out of airstrips too small for use by the C-130.

PFC. Michael Reams of Company "C," 1st Battalion, 3rd Marine Regiment, leads his M60 machine gun team through tall elephant grass on the side of a small hill during a search-and-destroy operation just south of the Demilitarized Zone.

Above: The smallest of the tactical airlifters used by the U.S. Air Force in the Vietnam War was the Fairchild C-123 Provider. Seen here is a C-123K, with two booster turbojets in nacelles under the outer wing panels for improved performance.

Right: One of the targets most favored by the Viet Cong was the fuel dump, which could be attacked with rockets, mortars, and even hand grenades. Here a fireman tackles a blaze caused by a communist attack at the Qui Nhon Tank Farm in March 1969.

communist forces on the move. Most of these activities were confined to the border areas of South Vietnam's four northernmost provinces. In the rest of South Vietnam, the war against the Viet Cong continued as a counterpoint to the steady increase in the tempo of "Vietnamization" and American withdrawal.

During 1970, the North Vietnamese managed to infiltrate an estimated 60,000 men into South Vietnam, and the distinction between the Viet Cong and the North Vietnamese army virtually ceased to exist. The lack of South Vietnamese recruits meant that the North Vietnamese predominated numerically in the Viet Cong, and the weapons, training, and equipment were basically those of the North Vietnamese army.

The Attack on Dak Seang

One of the largest efforts made by the communists during 1970 was the attack on the Special Forces' camp at Dak Seang, lying in a distant corner of Kontum province near the border with Cam-

bodia and Laos. The camp, home to a small Special Forces detachment and some 400 Montagnard irregulars, was attacked by 3,000 communists on April 1. The communists failed to overrun the camp in their initial assault, and as the defenders prepared to last out a communist siege with the aid of powerful air support, a 3,000-strong column of South Vietnamese was despatched for the relief of the camp. The exercise was seen as a major test for the success of "Vietnamization." The first South Vietnamese infantry battalion reached the camp on April 10, and the communists were then driven back. Even so, the fighting continued at Dak Seang and Dak Pek, a similar camp 17 miles farther south, over the next few weeks until the communists finally broke off the fighting.

Throughout Southeast Asia, the air war increased considerably in 1970. Although the bombing of North Vietnam had been ended in 1968, a large-scale reconnaissance effort was still being continued over that country. Early in 1970 there were a number of North Vietnamese efforts to stop these aircraft with fighters

Electronic warfare was widely used to defeat the efforts of the radars and associated weapons used by the North Vietnamese. This Grumman EA-6A Intruder electronic warfare machine is seen in front of the revetments used by the U.S. Marines' VMCJ-1 squadron. The fintop pod housed receiver antennae for the radar-detection system, and the jammer pods carried under the wings had small slipstream-driven propellers on their noses to power the generators supplying each such pod with electrical power.

A Bell UH-1D helicopter prepares to land and deliver supplies as men of the 2nd Battalion, 47th Infantry Regiment (Mechanized), 9th Infantry Division, watch from an M113 armored personnel carrier during operations in the Cha Lang and Sprok Memut district of Cambodia during May 1970.

and surface-to-air missiles. The U.S. Air Force retaliated with a number of major attacks; one of the largest took place on May 2, when more than 400 American aircraft struck at North Vietnamese targets, most of them missile sites and support installations.

Another notable "air" operation took place later in the year. On November 21, a force of volunteers, specially trained for this unique operation, was carried by helicopter to Son Tay, a camp less than 25 miles west of Hanoi, the North Vietnamese capital. American intelligence had indicated that a large number of American prisoners were held in the camp, but the rescue force found the camp empty. The only conclusions to be drawn were that the intelligence had been wrong, or that the creation of the rescue effort had taken so long that the prisoners had been moved and intelligence had failed to keep track of the fact.

The Focus Shifts to Cambodia

However, the most important events of 1970 took place not in either Vietnam, but in Cambodia, South Vietnam's western neighbor. The country was ruled by Prince Norodom Sihanouk, who had made strenuous and generally successful efforts to maintain the neutrality of his country by making concessions to each side, most notably to the North Vietnamese whose so-called Sihanouk Trail stretched from the port of Kompong Som through the eastern regions of Cambodia into the southwestern part of South Vietnam. As with the earlier Ho Chi Minh Trail, the Sihanouk Trail was made up of a network of waterways, roads, bicycle tracks, and footpaths under the control of the Viet Cong. During the later 1960s, the trail was expanded as the core of a communist base area, complete with training establishments, staging and rest areas, and dumps of various types. Located close to the South Vietnamese frontier, but still clearly within neutral Cambodia, these areas were called communist sanctuaries by the allies, and during 1969 they were vastly expanded as part of the overall communist scheme to keep their major forces out of South Vietnam until the departure of the U.S. forces.

By 1970, allied intelligence suggested that the communist forces in Cambodia amounted to a garrison of some 5,000 Viet Cong and North Vietnamese combat soldiers and 40,000 support troops, together with many thousands more troops either waiting in the region or passing through on their way to their operational areas. In real terms, this gave the Viet Cong and North Vietnamese effective control over the eastern and northeastern parts of Cambodia.

The North Vietnamese and the Viet Cong maintained diplomatic ties with the Cambodian government in Phnom Penh, but nevertheless suffered fluctuations in the warmth of their relationships with Sihanouk's government. Not until 1966 did this government admit that there were foreign troops on its soil, and a tacit agreement yielded much of the country's sparsely populated eastern regions to the communists, guaranteeing that there were few clashes between Cambodian forces and their "guests": indeed, in the period between 1963 and 1970, the Cambodian forces suffered only about 1,000 casualties in clashes with the Viet Cong and the North Vietnamese.

Growth of Communist Strength in Cambodia

The allies found it difficult to get reliable information about communist dispositions and strengths in this border region, which was poorly defined and peopled by Montagnards and ethnic Vietnamese. Between Saigon and Phnom Penh, the most distinctive feature of the border region was the so-called "Parrot's Beak," where a sliver of Cambodian territory some 15 miles wide and 25 miles deep jutted into South Vietnam. It was bisected by Route 1, the main communication link between the two capitals. This was a fertile plain, but to the north the border

Two men of Company "A," 1st Battalion, 27th Infantry Regiment, 25th Infantry Division, check the area around a burning communist "hootch" for documents during a search-and-destroy mission in the "Fish Hook" area of Cambodia on May 14, 1970.

Men of Troop "A," 3rd Squadron, 4th Cavalry Regiment, 25th Infantry Division, lurch through the Cambodian jungle on an M113 armored personnel carrier in a search-and-destroy operation in May 1970.

Lon Nol
For further references see pages 64, 78, 129

entered deep jungle as it turned northeast in a feature known as the "Dog's Face" near the town of Krek. The boundary then made another small projection, known as the "Fish Hook," into South Vietnam before running comparatively smoothly to the northeast and then north to the junction of Laos, Cambodia, and South Vietnam, northwest of the South Vietnamese city of Kontum. To the south of the "Parrot's Beak," the border ran west across the River Mekong and then veered south-west to the sea. Most of the communist sanctuaries lay in the region around the Mekong, in the "Parrot's Beak" and the "Fish Hook," while smaller sanctuaries were located in the border region throughout northeastern Cambodia and southeastern Laos as far north as the 17th parallel.

During December 1967, the Cambodians became more worried about the geographical extent and numerical strength of the communist presence in the country. Sihanouk announced that the communist sanctuaries in his country were there without official permission. At the same time, the prince indicated that he would have no objections to incursions into Cambodia by U.S. forces involved in "hot pursuit" of communist forces fleeing from South Vietnam. This permission was later extended to U.S. aircraft, which were now allowed to strike at communist sanctuaries in Cambodia. It was later revealed by the Department of Defense that the U.S. Air Force had secretly flown no fewer than 3,630 B-52 Stratofortress heavy-bomber raids against targets inside Cambodia before March 1970.

Sihanouk Overthrown by Lon Nol

By this time, Sihanouk had become seriously concerned that the communist buildup along Cambodia's eastern frontier was a threat to his country. He traveled to Moscow to try to persuade the Soviets to put pressure on the Viet Cong and North Vietnamese. However, during his absence, Sihanouk was deposed and replaced by Lieutenant General Lon Nol,

Men of Troop "H," 11th Armored Cavalry Regiment, take a break during operations north of Snoul during the Cambodian incursion of May 1970.

commander of the Cambodian army. The general immediately informed the United States and South Vietnamese that Cambodia was now firmly on their side and closed Cambodian ports to the communists. Unfortunately for the allies, though, the general was a wholly inadequate ruler. By early April, Cambodia was in the throes of a full-scale war between the Cambodian army and the Viet Cong, with other factions joining sides whenever they saw a particular opportunity for themselves. The situation was made worse by atrocities committed by both the Cambodian army and Cambodian civilian groups against Vietnamese living in their country. In the short term the only countries to aid Lon Nol were South Vietnam and Thailand.

By the end of April, it was clear that the small Cambodian army was no match for the battle-experienced Viet Cong and their Cambodian communist allies, who controlled most of rural Cambodia north and east of Phnom Penh. By May, the government forces had been driven back into the

major cities, and Phnom Penh was under virtual siege.

In the middle of April, the Nixon administration decided to take a hand and launched a program of aid for Lon Nol. At the same time, the Military Assistance Command, Vietnam, was given permission to plan a series of incursions into Cambodia to destroy the communist sanctuaries nestled along the border with South Vietnam. These raids were planned with the double objective of easing the pressure that the communists were exerting on Lon Nol's forces, and reducing the longer-term threat to the allied forces in South Vietnam. As the Americans were planning their first operation, the South Vietnamese launched the initial incursion on April 14 with a sweep through the "Angel's Wing" region.

Allied Operations into Cambodia

On April 29, the South Vietnamese started what was in effect a full-scale invasion. Twelve thousand A.R.V.N. troops, with large numbers of American advisers, moved up Route 1 to attack communist positions in the "Parrot's Beak" area. On May 1, a somewhat larger force of American and South Vietnamese troops crossed the border into the "Fish Hook" area near the towns of Mimot and Snoul. On May 4, the offensive was extended far to the north; a comparatively small American and South Vietnamese task force probed over the frontier and advanced into the Se Sam valley. Two days later, another three areas were added to the cross-border offensive: the "Dog's Face," the region northeast of the "Fish Hook" near the town of Loc Ninh, and the region north of the regional capital of Phuoc Binh. Two days later still, on May 8, the final component was added to this large-scale allied operation when South Vietnamese forces pushed up the line of the River Mekong to enter the "Parrot's Beak" from the south.

Of these many incursions, the largest and most important in the tactical sense were those into the "Parrot's Beak" and the "Fish Hook," for allied possession of these areas would safeguard Saigon from a major communist attack and ease the South Vietnamese task of protecting the III and IV Corps Tactical Zones of South Vietnam's southern regions.

The major South Vietnamese effort in the "Parrot's Beak" area was coordinated by Lieutenant General Do Cao Tri, commander of III Corps. Realizing the overall ineptitude of the politically appointed divisional commanders under him, Tri left them out of his planning and dealt directly with the three relevant divisions. The result could have been a model for the "Vietnamization" program. Tri organized a strike force based on three armored cavalry squadrons equipped with M41 light tanks and M113 armored personnel carriers, two infantry regiments each deploying two rifle battalions, and a

Men of Troop "C," 11th Armored Cavalry Regiment, prepare for action after making contact with communist forces about 6 miles northwest of Mimot late in May 1970.

Men of Company "A," 1st Battalion, 5th Infantry Regiment, 1st Cavalry Division (Airmobile), prepare to move out and secure a communist arms cache discovered during the Cambodian incursion.

ranger group headquarters with two ranger battalions. Tri organized these units into three highly mobile task forces, each headed by a regimental headquarters and including one armored cavalry squadron and two infantry or ranger battalions, supported by U.S. or South Vietnamese light artillery.

As the offensive continued, Tri replaced weary battalions with fresh units, thereby keeping the task forces up to strength. At longer intervals, he replaced the one ranger and two infantry headquarters with fresh headquarters, which brought with them their own battalions. This meant that from highest to lowest level, both commanders and troops were as fresh as possible, and the rotation also meant that as many units as possible could gain combat experience. To a lesser extent, the practice was followed by other South Vietnamese commanders; the effect was overall success in this small campaign, as well as a general improvement in the combat experience, and thus

the fighting skills, of many South Vietnamese units.

South Vietnamese Successes

Tri established his operational command post at the provincial capital of Tay Ninh, between the "Parrot's Beak" and "Fish Hook" areas, but generally left his staff to coordinate matters there while he exercised field command from a number of locations closer to the front line within Cambodia. In three days, Tri's forces had swept right through their operational area behind spearheads of infantry riding on armored fighting vehicles. But the results were disappointing because the communists had learned of the forthcoming operation and, knowing the futility of standing and fighting technically superior forces, had melted away into Cambodian regions too far from the frontier to be considered within the scope of permitted "hot pursuit" operations. The South

The air war was much different from ground combat. Colonal Olds describes air-to-air combat against enemy MiG jet fighters over North Vietnam.

At the onset of this battle, the MIG's popped up out of the clouds. Unfortunately, the first one to pop through came up at my 6 o'clock position. I think this was more by chance than design. As it turned out, within the next few moments, many others popped out of the clouds in varying positions around the clock.

I broke left, turning just hard enough to throw off his deflection, waiting for my three and four men to slice in on him. At the same time I saw another MIG pop out of the clouds in a wide turn about my 11 o'clock position, a mile and a half away. I went after him and ignored the one behind me. I fired a missile at him just as he disappeared into the clouds.

I'd seen another pop out in my 10 o'clock position, going from my right to left; in other words, just about across the circle from me. When the first MIG I fired at disappeared, I slammed full afterburner and pulled in hard to gain position on the second MIG. I pulled the nose up high about 45 degrees, inside his circle. Mind you, he was turning around to the left so I pulled the nose up high and rolled to the right. I got up on top of him and half upside down, hung there, and waited for him to complete more of his turn and timed it so that as I continued to roll down behind him, I'd be about 20 degrees angle off and about 4,500 to 5,000 feet behind him. That's exactly what happened. Frankly, I am not sure he ever saw me. When I got down low and behind, and he was outlined by the sun against a brilliant blue sky, I let him have two sidewinders, one of which hit and blew his right wing off.

Another pilot in the same battle recalls:

At approximately 1504 hours my flight was attacked by three MIG-21's, two from 10 o'clock high and one, simultaneously, from 6 o'clock low. I did not see the MIG at 6 o'clock at first, as I had already started to counter the attack of the two closing from the front quarter. My rear seat pilot called me (very urgently), stating a MIG was closing from 6 o'clock and was in missile firing range on my number three and four aircraft. I was a bit hesitant to break

off the attack I already had started on the other two MIG's as I had just seen Olds flight pass underneath us a few seconds before and I had a fleeting thought that this was who my rear seater was seeing. However, I quickly max rolled form a left bank to a steep right and observed the low MIG as called. I called a hard right break for 03 and 04. As they executed, the MIG broke left for some strange reason, and for a split second was canopy-to-canopy with me. I could clearly see the pilot and the bright read star markings.

I immediately started a barrel roll to gain separation for attack and fired one Sidewinder. As he accelerated rapidly and broke harder left, my missile missed, but he broke right into the flight path of my number two aircraft, flown by Capt. Everett T. Raspberry. I called Captain Raspberry and told him to press the attack as the two aircraft that I had initially engaged had now swung around into a range, head-on. I had a good missile growl and fired two AIM-9's in rapid succession at them. I immediately rolled over to reposition in fighting wing position on my number two, Captain Raspberry. It was during this maneuver that I saw an F-4, which was Olds lead, blast the wing off another MIG in another fight in progress a few miles from us.

I continued down with Captain Raspberry and remembered thinking he was getting a little inside optimum missile parameters. He then executed a rolling maneuver, placing him in perfect position.

Raspberry was flying with 1st Lt. Robert W. Western in Ford 02 during the encounter, when they rolled in for the fourth victory in Operation Bolo:

The maneuver positioned my aircraft at the MIG's 6 o'clock at a range of approximately 3,500 feet in a left turn. I assume that the MIG pilot was not aware of my position because he rolled out of his turn, placing me in a perfect position to fire the AIM-9B. I fired the Sidewinder and observed the missile home up his tailpipe. As soon as the missile detonated the MIG-21 swapped ends and stalled out. The aircraft went into a slow spiral, falling towards the undercast.

Vietnamese did capture large quantities of supplies that the communists had not been able to evacuate and, in the few actions that were fought, performed creditably on the field of battle.

Just as important, the very fact that they had left their own region and taken the war to the communists did wonders for the morale of the South Vietnamese.

On the other side of the coin, however, the operation also revealed a number of failings in the South Vietnamese forces. At the planning level, the earlier launch of the sweep through the "Angel's Wing" area gave the communists warning of what was about to happen. At an operational level, the four helicopter squadrons available to the South Vietnamese army were deployed on other tasks and were therefore not available to

provide Tri's men with tactical mobility and aerial fire support. Another failing was the use of corps and divisional artillery for area security duties, which meant that the job of providing artillery support fell on American heavy artillery units inside South Vietnam. Other support was provided by U.S. tactical aircraft and helicopters.

U.S. Involvement in the Cambodian Incursions

The first major U.S. involvement in the offensive's ground fighting began on May 1, when the 1st Cavalry Division (Airmobile) partnered the South Vietnamese Airborne Division in an operation into the "Fish Hook." The two formations had

Men of Troop "C," 3rd Squadron, 4th Cavalry Regiment, move their M113 armored personnel carriers and, in the background, an M551 Sheridan light tank, into line for a sweep through the Krek rubber plantation on May 22, 1970.

Surrounded by stacked ammunition at Fire Support Base "Triple Deuce" in South Vietnam, M109 self-propelled howitzers fire their 155-mm (6.1-inch) caliber howitzers on communist positions deep inside Cambodia during May 1970.

been working side by side for several months, but had a hard task ahead of them. They were committed to capture COSVAN, or the Central Office for South Vietnam, the headquarters controlling the Viet Cong throughout Indochina. The job was made harder by the fact that the "Fish Hook" region was heavily forested, making air support more difficult.

Overall command was entrusted to Brigadier General Robert M. Shoemaker, the 1st Cavalry Division's assistant division commander for maneuver. His Task Force Shoemaker included the U.S. division's 3rd Brigade (reinforced with tanks and mechanized infantry), the 11th Armored Cavalry Regiment, and the South Vietnamese division's 3rd Airborne Brigade. Shoemaker's plan was for the

Americans to advance into the "Fish Hook" from the east, south, and west to drive the communists against the South Vietnamese brigade's three battalions, which would have been helicopter-ferried into positions along the northern side of the "Fish Hook" before advancing south to link up with the Americans and complete the entrapment of the communists. Artillery support was provided by heavy batteries located in South Vietnam, and by lighter batteries airlifted into the landing zones once they had been secured. All ranks appreciated that success would come only from initial surprise, followed by fast-moving ground operations.

The offensive started early on May 1 with a heavy artillery bombardment and concentrated attacks by B-52

Opposite: The men and M113 armored personnel carriers of the 11th Armored Cavalry Regiment receive a friendly welcome from Cambodian children as they move through a village about 5 miles northeast of Mimot in May, 1970.

Below: A Chinook helicopter prepares to land at Landing Zone "Bronco" and evacuate men wounded during the Cambodian incursion.

Stratofortress heavy bombers. The 94 pieces of artillery included four 203-mm (8-inch), six 175-mm (6.89-inch), and 44 155-mm (6·1-inch) weapons, and fired a total of 2,436 rounds within the first day's delivery of 5,460 rounds. The air effort included 36 bomber and 185 tactical air support missions, and landing zones for the South Vietnamese blocking force were cleared by dropping 15,000-pound (6,804-kg) bombs fused to detonate about seven feet above the ground to blast a circular clearing in the forest.

The offensive's first action came at about 7:40 a.m., when Bell AH-1 HueyCobra helicopter gunships destroyed a North Vietnamese truck. In general, communist opposition was light, and none

of the South Vietnamese 3rd Airborne Brigade's landings was opposed. The allies were confident that the attack had been a complete surprise, and this confidence became a certainty when they realized that the communists were actively seeking to avoid a major engagement. Instead, they were dividing into small groups and parties that tried to filter out of the allied trap. Most of the little fighting that did occur happened when communist parties were flushed into open areas by the advancing allied ground forces and then attacked by the circling AH-1 HueyCobras. The only heavy casualties suffered by the allies were those of the South Vietnamese 3rd Airborne Brigade, which was operating in unfamiliar terrain and stumbled onto

Above: South Vietnamese infantry board a U.S. Army "Huey" before an operation in the "Fish Hook" area of Cambodia during May 8, 1970.

Opposite Top: The fire-support version of the "Huey" utility helicopter was the Bell AH-1 HueyCobra. It had a slim fuselage for the crew of two, and carried rocket launchers and/or machine gun pods on the four hardpoints under its stub wings.

Opposite Below: High tactical mobility by helicopter was one of the great military advances of the Vietnam War.

communist mines and barrages of light mortar fire laid down by the communist rearguards.

The Communists Suffer Heavy Materiel Losses

Though the offensive failed to trap large numbers of communists, it was otherwise successful. On May 3, U.S. forces entered Mimot, and two days later, allied sodiers occupied Snoul. On May 5, American forces stumbled onto the communists' vast bunker complex known as "The City." Analysis later revealed that this was the headquarters and supply depot for the North Vietnamese 7th Infantry Division. Careful examination revealed that "The City" contained 182 large bunkers (used for the storage of varied weapons, ammunition, clothing, food, and medical supplies), 18 mess halls, and other features such as a small farm, barracks, and comprehensive training and classroom facilities. Weapons and equipment captured in "The City" included 1,282 small arms, 202 crew-served weapons, more than 1.5 million rounds of small arms ammunition, 58,000 pounds of plastic explosive, 22 cases of antipersonnel mines, 26.8 tons of rice, and 7.2 tons of corn. Other complexes were found in different parts of the allies' operational area, many of which were specialist dumps for items such as communication equipment and vehicle spares. The allies seized more than 300 vehicles; although most were trucks, there were also a Mercedes-Benz limousine and a Porsche sports car.

What the allies failed to find was COSVAN, which was thought to have a personnel strength of 2,400 as well as vast quantities of documentation. In common with most of the communist troops, COSVAN clearly escaped the allied net and filtered away to still more remote sanctuaries deeper in Cambodia.

By the middle of May, the two remaining brigades of the 1st Cavalry Division (Airmobile), together with the

South Vietnamese 9th Infantry Regiment were deeply involved in similar operations slightly farther to the northeast, in the "Fish Hook" region. In the pattern of such operations, the communists managed to avoid direct confrontation with the allies by falling back deeper into Cambodia, so the main activity of the allied troops was finding and cataloging communist bunker complexes. On May 8, for example, the 1st Cavalry Division's 2nd Brigade uncovered a complex known as "Rock Island East" that contained 293.75 tons of munitions. Despite the number of complexes discovered, allied commanders were sure that they represented at most only half of the complexes located in the border area of Cambodia.

Although the capture of communist supplies was valuable, it would have been foolhardy to imagine that this was a decisive blow against the enemies of South Vietnam: in time, the communists would make good these losses. So the best result that could be claimed for the Cambodian incursions was that they had bought more time for the policy of "Vietnamization" to be implemented fully.

The Fury of the American Public

Altogether more significant than the military results of the incursions themselves was American public reaction. Up to the time of the raids, public opposition

An M113 armored personnel carrier of the 2nd Battalion, 47th Infantry Regiment, 9th Infantry Division, fords a Cambodian stream during operation in the Cha Lang and Sprok Memut region.

to the war had been lessened by the reduced rate of U.S. casualties in South Vietnam and the knowledge that the withdrawal of American troops was continuing. And on April 20, the virtual eve of the Cambodian incursions, it was revealed that 15,000 more Americans would be pulled back from South Vietnam by the spring of 1971.

News of the incursions revived the hostility of the American people for the administration, and the antiwar movement gained a new lease of life as it heaped its anger on President Nixon, his administration, and the Department of Defense. To the antiwar movement, the Cambodian incursions were a clear attempt by Nixon and his military advisers to widen the scope of a war that was unwinnable and which most Americans thought was being abandoned. The movement therefore sponsored a wave of demonstrations and strikes across the country. Most passed off peacefully, but given the extent and high emotion of the protest, it was almost inevitable that there would be trouble somewhere.

Tragedy at Kent State University

The unfortunate spot was Kent State University in Ohio. Here violence flared as National Guardsmen opened fire and killed four students. The event focused the attention of the entire nation on the antiwar movement, which was seen as the victim of official brutality. The depth of hostility to the Vietnam War deepened, and in Congress a clear vote repealed the Gulf of Tonkin Resolution and instructed the president to recall all American forces from Cambodia by June 30.

The president protested that the incursions were in no way an effort to widen the scope of the war, but an attempt to ease the situation in South Vietnam and thus simplify the process of extracting the U.S. forces, but this cut no ice with the American people. In an effort to placate the public, the president announced further troop withdrawals and, during December, the banning of the more dangerous types of defoliant. Neither measure won back for the

president any of the popularity that had been lost by the Cambodian incursions.

Defoliants are chemical agents designed to make trees lose their leaves. The Americans made extensive use of such agents in South Vietnam to reduce the natural cover which the communists used so skillfully in the heavily forested border regions. Thus large areas of forest were denuded of their leaves in a wide-ranging program of aerial spraying. It soon became clear that the spraying was causing irreparable ecological damage, but it continued until it began to become clear that humans were also affected with health and genetic problems whose implications were not fully realized for some years to come. The use of "Agent Orange" and other defoliating agents thus remains one of the most controversial aspects of the entire American involvement in the Vietnam War.

Stop-and-Go Moves toward Peace

While civil and international war swept into Cambodia in the spring and early summer of 1970, the search for peace was proceeding only with halting steps. Throughout 1969, the negotiations in Paris had been stalemated by North Vietnamese insistence that no settlement was possible until all "foreign" troops had been pulled out of South Vietnam, and also by North Vietnam's steadfast refusal to agree on what would constitute an "acceptable" government in South Vietnam. The main American negotiator was Henry Cabot Lodge, a two-time U.S. ambassador in South Vietnam, who insisted that the government of President Thieu would have to be involved in any meaningful settlement, but the North Vietnamese and the National Liberation Front united in demanding the creation of a coalition government in South Vietnam. In an effort to force the issue, the National Liberation Front announced, on June 10, the creation of a new Provisional Revolutionary Government at an unspecified location within South Vietnam as a rival to the Saigon government. Two days later, a delegation from this Provisional Revolution-

ary Government replaced the National Liberation Front delegation at the talks. The Provisional Revolutionary Government put itself forward as a broad-based administration recognizing the interests of South Vietnamese democratic, ethnic minority, and religious groups: the Saigon government refused to deal in any way with this communist front organization, but American negotiators accepted it to the talks, and events remained stalemated.

In July, President Thieu suggested that free South Vietnamese elections might be held with full participation of the National Liberation Front, but the communists quickly rejected the notion on the grounds that the present South Vietnamese government would be able to rig the electoral process. At this point, internal dissension again reared its head in South Vietnam. Vice President Ky also objected to Thieu's plan and said

that the armed forces would never permit the installation of any South Vietnamese government that included the communists.

Matters rested there through most of 1970. The Americans refused to budge from the position that no further progress could be made until a coalition administration had been sworn in after free elections organized by the Thieu government. Throughout the second half of 1970, the American negotiators offered a number of permutations based on the coalition government theme, but none was acceptable to the communists. In September, the communists offered to release all prisoners-of-war in exchange for elections supervised by a coalition government and for a deadline by which all U.S. forces would leave South Vietnam. The Americans responded in October with a five-point plan that included a ceasefire based on the current

A 105-mm (4·13-inch) caliber howitzer of the 2nd Battalion, 5th Cavalry Regiment, fires in support of friendly forces from Fire Support Base ''Anna'' during June 1970.

military situation, a two-sided release of prisoners-of-war, and negotiation about U.S. troop withdrawals.

Neither side found the other's position satisfactory, and in the following months, both parties made small concessions designed to whet the other's appetite. The communists agreed to international supervision of any elections that might be held in South Vietnam, but refused to agree with the ceasefire proposal on the ground that President Thieu wrongly claimed control over 99 percent of the population of South Vietnam. By this time the Americans' chief negotiator was David K.E. Bruce, who attempted to stimulate rational negotiation with the suggestion that the Americans might produce a definitive timetable for U.S. withdrawals if the North Vietnamese produced a comparable timetable for their own evacuation of the country.

None of the proposals from either side made any real inroad into the deadlocked nature of the negotiations, and world opinion began to conclude that the talks were being used by each side as a forum for its own propaganda.

Continued Operations in Cambodia

In Southeast Asia, meanwhile, U.S. involvement continued. The war in South Vietnam continued as before, but the ingredient now added to the equation was the anticommunist coalition's attempt to preserve the Lon Nol regime by both direct and indirect means. On April 25, 1970, the Nixon administration started a program of direct military assistance, initially with the delivery of ex-World War II weapons (small arms, machine guns, and ammunition) and supplies valued at $7.5 million. In a comparable program, the South Vietnamese government supplied large quantities of captured communist weapons, including AK-47 assault rifles, and sent a team of

A Lockheed C-130 Hercules tactical transport arrives at Plei Djerang in Cambodia on May 14, 1970, with a load of supplies and reinforcements from South Vietnam.

advisers to Phnom Penh. These allied efforts ignored the fact that Lon Nol's need was not for weapons, but for adequately trained troops led by capable commanders and exhibiting a high level of motivation.

On May 1, men of ethnic Cambodian origins, trained by the U.S. Army's Special Forces, made an unsuccessful attempt to open a river passage to Phnom Penh up the River Mekong. On May 8, this objective was achieved by a large flotilla of American and South Vietnamese riverine craft. This could be only a temporary measure, however, and on May 14, Tri despatched one of his mechanized task forces from the "Parrot's Beak" area up Route 1 to the Cambodian capital, re-establishing overland communication between the anticommunist faction in Cambodia with South Vietnam.

On May 9, American and South Vietnamese naval forces established a blockade line about 100 miles off the Cambodian coast to prevent the arrival of communist reinforcements and supplies on Cambodia's southern coast. At the same time, the U.S. air forces in Southeast Asia were granted permission to fly missions in support of the Cambodian ground forces, although such missions were claimed as part of the continuing interdiction program rather than any separate help for the Lon Nol regime.

Even so, the forces loyal to Lon Nol were forced to fall back from the rural areas toward Cambodia's main towns and cities throughout this period. With the indirect aid of the U.S. and South Vietnamese cross-border incursions, which tied down large numbers of communist troops even though there was no severe fighting, Lon Nol's forces were now able to stabilize the position to a significant degree, although both sides realized that this was only a temporary situation. The Cambodian leader realized that effective offensive action was the only key to success. He rapidly expanded his army to 100,000 and then 200,000 men, but his new "soldiers" were poorly trained and, more important, lacked motivation to a high degree. They performed adequately in defensive operations, but showed an alarming tendency to disintegrate during offensive ones. The Americans tried unsuccessfully to make a contribution with a force of Cambodian mercenaries trained in South Vietnam by the Special Forces.

The Communists Bide their Time

The communists at this time failed to press their advantage, perhaps fearing that the war might acquire ethnic overtones as a conflict between the historically antagonistic Cambodians and Vietnamese. More probably, they were worried that success in Cambodia might tempt the Americans into slowing the pace of their departure from Southeast Asia. Instead, the Vietnamese communists played a waiting game, concentrating their efforts on not winning the war directly but on developing the political and military strength of the Cambodian communists.

In accordance with the congressional directive, U.S. forces were withdrawn from Cambodia by the end of June, but South Vietnamese forces continued to operate in Cambodia. Their objectives were to keep the surviving communists off balance in the border region, prevent the reestablishment of sanctuaries in the border region, and maintain communication with Phnom Penh along Route 1 and the Mekong. Later in 1970, the South Vietnamese added to their objectives the clearing of Route 4, the highway linking Phnom Penh with Kompong Som, the port that was Cambodia's most important commercial city. The key to Route 4 was the provincial capital of Kompong Speu, halfway between Phnom Penh and Kompong Som; on June 13 the city fell to the Viet Cong. Just three days later, a combined South Vietnamese and Cambodian force recaptured the place, which was the farthest point into Cambodia reached by the South Vietnamese. Between June 24 and 26, the communists made a determined effort to regain Kompong Speu, but were unsuccessful. Even so, the communists kept a grip on other parts of Route 4, so communications between Phnom Penh and Kompong Som were still impossible.

Further problems for Lon Nol's govern-

ment came on June 17, when communist forces cut the sole railroad line between Phnom Penh and Thailand. This left the routes to South Vietnam as the Cambodian government's only links with the rest of the world.

During 1971, the communist forces felt strong enough to resume the offensive and during the year, they made decisive inroads into the areas held by Lon Nol's government. The Cambodian forces were driven back toward Phnom Penh, and the South Vietnamese pulled back toward their own frontier. In the three years from 1972 to late 1974, the communist forces exerted inexorable pressure, and by the beginning of 1975 Lon Nol's forces were confined largely to Phnom Penh. Eventually, a last-minute U.S. air effort (large quantities of tactical air support and the delivery of supplies) could not prevent the fall of Phnom Penh on April 17, 1975, just two weeks before the communist capture of Saigon.

The Laotian Factor

From 1963, it became clear that one of the keys to success in the fighting for South Vietnam was control of Laos, for along its border areas, the Ho Chi Minh Trail debouched into South Vietnam. American planning for Laos was thus based on two hopes: severing the Ho Chi Minh Trail and denying the communists any effective use of Laos. Although there were compelling military reasons to aim at both these objectives, U.S. strategists also felt that denying Laos to the communists would not only aid South Vietnam but safeguard Thailand.

These objectives notwithstanding, North Vietnam maintained a secret force of some 100,000 men in Laos between 1963 and 1971. This considerable military strength not only guaranteed unhindered access to the Ho Chi Minh Trail, but also supported (and indeed controlled) the Laotian communists, or the Pathet Lao, which was involved in an effort to topple the monarchy government that was seeking to keep Laos neutral in the spreading Southeast Asian war. It was clearly to the allies' advantage to check these communist plans, and the U.S. therefore supplied Laos with financial aid, advisers, and an increasing measure of

An 81-mm (3·2-inch) caliber mortar of the 1st Cavalry Division (Airmobile) returns communist fire during the Cambodian incursion.

79

tactical air support. To match the North Vietnamese support of the Pathet Lao, the Central Intelligence Agency secretly aided Major General Vang Pao's antiguerrilla army of 30,000 men, most of them Meo tribesmen.

Warfare in Laos was dominated by the annual weather cycle: in the dry season between November and April, the North Vietnamese and Pathet Lao communist forces struck out from their jungle sanctuaries in the eastern part of Laos to take Bolovens Plateau in the south, the panhandle region in the center, and the Plain of Jars in the north; then in the wet season between May and October, the complex array of anticommunist forces (royalists, neutralists, and Meo tribesmen) moved forward, with U.S. air support, to recapture the areas lost in the dry season.

Knock-On Effect from Cambodia

This neat pattern of cyclical operations was finally disrupted by the fall of Sihanouk's Cambodian government in March 1970. With the Sihanouk Trail now effectively denied to them, the North Vietnamese decided in the later part of 1970 to expand the Ho Chi Minh Trail as a way of regaining the capacity lost with the Sihanouk Trail. They had made considerable progress before the U.S. and South Vietnamese governments decided to intervene.

At this time, the North Vietnamese had in the panhandle region of Laos the equivalent of three infantry divisions with some 18,000 men, tanks, field artillery, and antiaircraft guns. By October 1970, the North Vietnamese had considerable experience of the awesome capabilities of U.S. air power. This experience had been gained in South Vietnam, where American air power was a major factor in the ground fighting, and in Laos, where a lengthy tactical and technical war had been waged as U.S. aircraft sought to find and destroy communist transport moving on the Ho Chi Minh Trail. During the second half of 1970, the communist forces in Laos therefore set up their antiaircraft guns in concentric rings covering the most likely sites for American and South Vietnamese airborne and heliborne landing under cover of conventional support aircraft and helicopter gunships. The scale of the operations that the communists expected is indicated by the quantity of supplies that flowed into this vital region: in the previous five years it had been 17,860 tons. In the period between September 1970 and February 1971, it totaled 23,200 tons. Such a buildup could not be completely concealed, and to the Americans, it suggested the possibility of a major offensive in the forthcoming dry season. The

This marine of the 3rd Marine Division keeps watch as he is silhouetted by the rising sun during Operation "Scotland II Truesdale North."

two most likely objectives would be the northeastern corner of Cambodia or the northwestern provinces of South Vietnam. In this region, the communist effort was coordinated by the North Vietnamese 70B Corps, which commanded the North Vietnamese 304th, 308th, and 320th Infantry Divisions, two regiments of artillery, and one regiment of tanks.

In December 1970, President Nixon instructed Admiral John S. McCain, Jr., the Commander in Chief, Pacific, to request from Abrams a plan for a preemptive strike into Laos. The U.S. commanders would have preferred to use American troops for the task, but after the Cambodian incursions, Congress had prohibited the use of U.S. ground forces in Cambodia and Laos, so South Vietnam would have to furnish the necessary soldiers. It was January 1971 before President Thieu gave the necessary permission. He designated the town of Tchepone, some 22 miles inside Laos, as the maximum permissible extent of South Vietnamese advance. The Congressional veto did not apply to American logistic support and air power,

A member of the Kit Carson Scouts fires an M60 machine gun on a sweep near Minh Tanh with Company "B," 2nd Battalion (Mechanized), 2nd Infantry Regiment, 1st Infantry Division, during February 1970.

so it was agreed that these would be furnished on a lavish scale.

A Major American and South Vietnamese Effort

Detailed planning of the ground operation was entrusted to Lieutenant General Hoang Xuan Lam's South Vietnamese I Corps, which was allocated the elite Airborne Division and Marine Brigade in addition to its own forces. The I Corps formations selected for the operation were the 1st Infantry Division, the 1st Armored Brigade, and a three-battalion ranger group. Tchepone, the point of farthest permissible South Vietnamese advance, lay on the junction of Route 9 and the Ho Chi Minh Trail, and had been selected as the final objective in the belief that its capture would sever the Ho Chi Minh Trail and thereby completely disrupt the dry-season operations that the communists were preparing. With American support, Lam planned the offensive as a westward advance from the Lang Vei area on three axes, covering a width some 19 miles from north to south: the 1st Armored Brigade was to advance west along Route 9, the ranger and airborne battalions were to move by helicopter along the hills north of Route 9, and the 1st Infantry Division was to be transported by helicopter along the escarpment above the River Xe Pon, which flows parallel with Route 9 on its southern side. The marine battalions were to be kept in reserve. The South Vietnamese part of the operation was named "Lam Son 719" after a famous Vietnamese victory over the Chinese in 1427 A.D., while the U.S. component was "Dewey Canyon II."

U.S. Air Power Supports South Vietnamese Ground Forces

Operation "Lam Son 719/Dewey Canyon II" was conceived as a four-phase

A radioman of the 1st Battalion, 22nd Infantry Regiment, 4th Infantry Division, stands guard over two communist prisoners as other men of his unit move supplies.

Hoang Xuan Lam
For further references see pages 83, 86, 88

An M60 machine gunner of Company ''B,'' 2nd Infantry Regiment, 1st Infantry Division, fires his weapon at a Viet Cong bunker encountered on February 27, 1970, during a sweep near Minh Tanh.

offensive. In the first phase, to be undertaken from January 30, American and South Vietnamese forces would clear Route 9 from the central part of Quang Tri province to the Laotian frontier, paying particular attention to possible ambush sites and the likelihood of mines, so that the South Vietnamese forces could concentrate at Khe Sanh before moving up to Lang Vei. In the second phase, 16,000 South Vietnamese soldiers would advance on Tchepone. In the third phase, the South Vietnamese forces would consolidate in the Tchepone area and destroy all communist dumps discovered in an intensive search operation. The fourth phase would begin on March 10 (or perhaps slightly later, depending on

the strength of the communist opposition), and the South Vietnamese would fall back into their own country.

The U.S. contribution was provided by XXIV Corps, the largest American formation in the I Corps Tactical Zone. The corps commander was Lieutenant General James W. Sutherland, who assisted Lam in the planning phase of the operation, and the units he allocated to the offensive were an artillery group, an engineer group, a combat aviation battalion, and a military police battalion from his corps troops; two brigades of infantry, three battalions of artillery, and one combat aviation group from the 101st Airborne Division; the 1st Brigade of the 5th Mechanized Division; and the 11th

Many soldiers grew discouraged when increasing numbers of Americans joined the anti-war movement. Others continued to go above and beyond the call of duty:

JIMENEZ, JOSE FRANCISCO
Rank and organization:
Lance Corporal, United States Marine Corps, Company K, 3rd Battalion, 7th Marines, 1st Marine Division.
Place and date:
Quang Nam Province, Republic of Vietnam, 28th August 1969.
Entered service at: *Phoenix, Ariz.*
Date and place of birth:
March 20, 1946, Mexico City, Mexico.
Citation:
For conspicuous gallantry and intrepidity at the risk of his life above and beyond the call of duty while serving as a Fire Team Leader with Company K, 3rd Battalion, 7th Marines, 1st Marine Division in operations against the enemy in the Republic of Vietnam on 28 August 1969. On that date Lance Corporal Jimenez' unit came under heavy attack by North Vietnamese Army soldiers concealed in well camouflaged emplacements. Lance Corporal Jimenez reacted by seizing the initiative and plunging forward toward the enemy positions. He personally destroyed several enemy personnel and silenced an antiaircraft weapon. Shouting encouragement to his companions, lance Corporal Jimenez continued his aggressive forward movement. He slowly manuevered to within ten feet of hostile soldiers who were firing automatic weapons from a trench and, in the face of vicious enemy fire, destroyed the position. Although he was by now the target of concentrated fire from hostile gunners intent upon halting his assault, Lance Corporal Jimenez continued to press forward. As he moved to attack another enemy soldier, he was mortally wounded. Lance Corporal Jimenez' indomitable courage, aggressive fighting spirit and unfaltering devotion to duty upheld the highest traditions of the Marine Corps and of the United States Naval Service.

Lance Corporal Jimenez received a posthumous Congressional Medal of Honor.

When the Americans departed the war the North Vietnamese launched a nationwide offensive. It failed in 1972. The results were different when they tried again in 1975. A North Vietnamese recalls.

A people who know how to arise and take up arms and wage a life-or-death war to liberate themselves from the yoke of slavery must also know how to conclude the war in the most advantageous way. Under the wise leadership of the party, we had sacrificed and fought staunchly and had signed the Paris Agreement in hopes of ending the war in an atmosphere of national reconciliation and concord and end U.S. Intervention with honor. But our enemies thought differently. They turned to an insidious plot intended to cause the war to "fade away" so that they could win complete victory. But in life, people who play with fire get burned. The United States was able to evaluate our fighting strength and courage, but it did not yet understand the cleverness and intelligence of the Vietnamese people, and thought that it could deceive us. If the legality of the agreement could not end the war, the only method would be the use of revolutionary violence. Our people were much in need of peace, but true peace that was tied in with freedom and national independence and was in accord with the conscience of mankind. With a strong sense of responsibility towards our people and the people of the world, the Political Bureau of the Party Central Committee issued a resolution calling for the completion of the national democratic revolution throughout our nation and the eventual unification of the homeland during the 1975-1976 period.

Brigade of the 23rd Infantry Division (Americal). The contribution was significant, totaling 10,000 troops, 2,000 fixed-wing aircraft, and 600 helicopters, though only the fixed- and rotary-wing aircraft were permitted to cross the Laotian frontier.

The offensive was scheduled to pass through mountainous and heavily forested terrain, which offered few places suitable for use as major helicopter landing zones. The weather in this late stage of the wet season included rain, low cloud, and fog, and the North Vietnamese understood that the U.S. pilots would have to operate at very low level. The North Vietnamese therefore placed large numbers of antiaircraft guns in the valleys that they thought most likely to be used by pilots trying to fly "under" the weather. Despite the strenuous efforts of the U.S. and South Vietnamese planners and logisticians, the preparations and movements of so many troops could not be

concealed effectively, and the North Vietnamese were aware of what was about to fall on them.

The Laotian Incursion Begins

Just after midnight on January 30, 1971, Operation "Lam Son 719/Dewey Canyon II" started. The allied force moved out toward Khe Sanh and Lang Vei, and initial progress was satisfactory. But on February 1, even before the first South Vietnamese troops crossed the Laotian frontier, the whole operation was denounced by China and the U.S.S.R. as a flagrant example of the American penchant for widening its "imperial war of aggression." During the next seven days, further strong disapproval came from the American antiwar movement headed by Senator Mike Mansfield, the Secretary-General of the United Nations Organization, and the government of Laos.

Truly heavy fire support was supplied by weapons such as the 8-inch (203-mm) caliber howitzer of this M110 self-propelled equipment of Battery "B," 6th Battalion, 27th Artillery Regiment, near Landing Zone "Hong" about 7½ miles northeast of Song Be in March 1970.

The second phase of the operation got underway in the mid-morning of February 8. As the 1st Armored Brigade crossed the frontier and advanced along Route 9, men of the airborne and ranger battalions established two fire bases on Laotian soil north of Route 9, while men of the 1st Infantry Division constructed two more fire bases on the escarpment above the Xe Pon. By dusk on the following day, the armored force had reached the village of Aloui, about halfway between the frontier and Tchepone.

Until then, the commander of the North Vietnamese 70B Corps had not reacted. Now sure that the allied operation was not a diversion intended to decoy his forces away from an invasion of Cambodia or even North Vietnam, he committed substantial forces. Elements of the three North Vietnamese divisions moved south to take the airborne and ranger battalions on their right flank with artillery, sapper, and infantry attacks. U.S. air support was made virtually impossible by the weather and by thick smoke from the artillery fire. By February 22, Ranger Base South had been surrounded by the North Vietnamese, whose heavy concentration of antiaircraft fire also made the aerial resupply of Ranger Base North impossible. In these circumstances, the rangers pulled back after suffering just under 300 casualties and claiming to have killed more than twice that number of North Vietnamese.

The Communist Riposte

By February 25, the South Vietnamese forces had pushed forward from Aloui. At this stage, the 500 men holding Airborne Objective 31 came under heavy attack from 2,000 North Vietnamese infantry supported by 20 PT-76 light tanks. With the help of U.S. tactical aircraft, the South Vietnamese airborne soldiers fought off two North Vietnamese attacks on this day, inflicting heavy losses on the enemy, and then held out for another three days of bitter attacks. Finally the airborne soldiers fought their way out of the North Vietnamese trap and moved south to link up with the armored force, while the North Viet-

namese captured 120 men including a battalion commander.

By March 1, the South Vietnamese had lost two of the fire bases on their northern flank, and another two were under siege. Lam decided to modify his operational plan to prevent his armored force being taken in the flank or having its line of communications cut. Lam accordingly ordered his armored, airborne, and ranger units to take up a defensive position along Route 9 and instructed the 1st Infantry Division to move on Tchepone via a series of landing zones along the southern escarpment west of Aloui. With the support of an American combat aviation battalion, the 1st Infantry Division created and used three landing zones as it moved well forward by March 5.

An Aerial Armada

March 6 was the day selected for the assault on Tchepone, and the scene was prepared by the bombing of the area by B-52 Stratofortress heavy bombers. Then two battalions of South Vietnamese infantry were delivered to Tchepone in 120 UH-1H "Huey" transport helicopters escorted by large numbers of AH-1 HueyCobra gunship helicopters from an American air cavalry squadron. The gunships poured masses of suppressive fire into the North Vietnamese defenses, and the transport armada lost only one machine shot down as it swooped in to deliver the infantrymen. Operating from Khe Sanh, 48 miles east of Tchepone, the helicopters completed the largest and longest-ranged heliborne tactical assault of the Vietnam War.

The troops encountered little opposition on the ground and were soon involved in consolidating their position and beginning the search for North Vietnamese dumps. Two days after the Tchepone landing, Abrams and Sutherland were able to announce that the operation was a complete success, and that the South Vietnamese had discovered enough rice to feed 159 communist battalions for one month, small arms to equip eight battalions, other weapons, ranging from machine guns to light artillery, to outfit nine battalions,

Pilot , 1st Marine Air Wing, U.S. Marine Corps, Vietnam, 1967

The aircraft of the U.S. Marine Corps' aviation arm were heavily involved in the air war over Vietnam and played the major part in supporting the marine ground formations fighting in the part of South Vietnam just south of the Demilitarized Zone. The core of this pilot's kit are the CS/FRP-1 flight coveralls in flame-resistant fabric, and though many pilots preferred jungle boots in case they had to eject and move across country on foot, this man sports standard brown flying boots. Other items of his equipment include B-3A flying gloves, the Z-4 anti-g suit, cutaway MA-2 torso harness, Mk 2 life preserver, APH-6D helmet, SV-1 survival vest complete with a shroud-cutting knife and radio, and RSSK-1 seat pack survival kit.

and 714 tons of ammunition. The South Vietnamese also revealed the fact that up to March 8 they had killed 7,100 communist soldiers.

Lam Orders the South Vietnamese Withdrawal

Worried about the onset of heavy rains and the possibility of a major counterattack by the reinforced North Vietnamese 70B Corps, Lam ordered his troops to begin their withdrawal on March 10. Over the next five days, the South Vietnamese were evacuated from Tchepone and their other position on Route 9, even though many units were still hotly engaged against North Vietnamese forces. This put the helicopters of the 101st Airborne Division under severe threat. Brigadier General Sidney B. Berry, Jr., the assistant division commander, ordered his pilots to pack into their machines as many South Vietnamese as possible and thereby

reduce the number of trips that they would have to make. The South Vietnamese construed this as the origins of a panic evacuation, and many machines staggered back to Khe Sanh with soldiers who had abandoned their positions to grab onto the skids of the helicopters.

The last battle of "Lam Son 719" was the North Vietnamese assault on Fire Base Delta, about 10 miles southeast of Aloui, on March 22. Here the South Vietnamese 147th Marine Battalion checked the North Vietnamese over a period of four hours before being lifted out by helicopter. The last South Vietnamese soldiers were evacuated from the Laotian panhandle on March 25 by helicopters of the 101st Airborne Combat Aviation Group, and the propaganda machines of both sides moved into high gear with accounts of complete victory. The North Vietnamese said that: "Typical of that total debacle was the sight of Saigon soldiers trying to cling to the choppers' skids, and being kicked

Otter vehicles of the U.S. Marine Corps navigate a river on patrol south of Cau Lu.

The soft terrain prevalent in many parts of South Vietnam was often a problem for the heavy vehicles operated by the American forces. Here mud and smoke fly as two linked M113 armored personnel carriers tow an M48A3 tank of Troop "A," 1st Squadron, 1st Cavalry Division, 25th Infantry Division (Americal), that had become stuck in the mud.

down by American airmen...The Americans ended by plastering grease on the skids...a fine picture of Vietnamization!" The North Vietnamese also claimed to have routed the "invasion," in the process killing, wounding, or capturing 16,400 men including 200 Americans. The South Vietnamese countered with the claim that they had killed 13,636 North Vietnamese for a mere 6,000 of their own men killed or wounded. U.S. estimates put the South Vietnamese casualty list at some 10,000 men, and American losses were 176 killed, 1,942 wounded, and 42 missing.

Mixed Results

What then was the real outcome of Operation "Lam Son 719/Dewey Canyon II"? The answer can only be found in an assessment of whether the South Vietnamese ground forces gained their two primary objectives of spoiling the North Vietnamese preparations for a spring offensive, and of proving the success of the "Vietnamization" policy by showing that the South Vietnamese forces could plan and conduct large-scale operations. As far as the first objective was concerned, the South Vietnamese had clearly won, for the North Vietnamese offensive in the Laotian panhandle was delayed by 12 months. There was more doubt about the second objective; the South Vietnamese had revealed both capabilities and failings: fighting skills had clearly improved, but planning and command had revealed severe limitations.

Opposite: Part of the heavy naval gunfire support for the U.S. forces operating in coastal regions of South Vietnam was provided by heavy cruisers dating from World War II. This is a view from a point on the forecastle of such a ship, with the 8-inch (203-mm) caliber guns of two triple turrets visible forward of the superstructure. In the foreground are empty powder canisters.

Problems in Northern Laos

Operation "Lam Son 719/Dewey Canyon II" had a serious effect on North Vietnamese plans for the Laotian panhandle and a lesser effect on operations in southern Laos, and North Vietnamese reinforcements were moved in to check the South Vietnamese advance on Tchepone. In northern Laos, however, the operation had little impact. The Communist forces continued to close in on Luang Prabang and Long Tieng, respectively the royalist capital and the major city of the Meo region.

The advance on Luang Prabang had started on February 2, the same day that the North Vietnamese and Pathet Lao took Muong Soui, a town just west of the Plain of Jars. The communist advance continued, and by March 20 six battalions closed to within mortar and rocket range of the Laotian capital. Moderately severe fighting continued until the arrival from Vientiane of another three government battalions, and the communists were then pushed back to the edge of the Plain of Jars, where sporadic fighting continued for the rest of the dry season.

Farther south, the communist forces approached Long Tieng between February 12 and 14. For the rest of the month, there was small-scale but bitter fighting as the communists failed to drive out the Meo force, despite the fact that the Meo were equipped for guerrilla, rather than regular, warfare and suffered some 700 casualties. The communist siege was eventually broken by a relief force of three Laotian battalions and four battalions of Thai volunteers despatched from Luang Prabang on March 6. The communists pulled back to the hills overlooking Long Tieng from the east, and Vang Pao completed preparations from his annual rainy-season offensive.

The U.S. was becoming tired of the inconclusive, seesaw nature of the seasonal fighting in Laos and decided to reduce the level of aid for the country. In the spring of 1971, for example, Abrams ordered that the number of air support missions flown over Laos should be cut by half from July of that year. This left a monthly total of 11,750 missions, of which 70 percent were allocated to the southern and central regions, the areas most important to the North Vietnamese because they contained the sections of the Ho Chi Minh Trail feeding into South Vietnam. The remaining 30 percent of missions were allocated to the Royal Laotian Army and the Meo guerrillas, which could thus rely on only 32 instead of the former 60 sorties a day.

The Meo Offensive Makes an Early Start

Warned by his Central Intelligence Agency advisers of the forthcoming cut in the level of U.S. air support he would receive, Vang Pao decided to start his rainy-season offensive earlier than normal so that he would receive the maximum possible air support before the reduction on July 1. The offensive began on April 15, and through a skillful combination of frontal attacks and decoy moves, the Meo forces gradually drove back the communists, who nevertheless remained a longer-term threat to Long Tieng. In an effort to force them to fall back, Vang Pao arranged for 700 of his troops to be helicopter-carried to Phou Seu on the Plain of Jars, where they threatened the line of communication between the forward-deployed communist forces and their base area. It was not until June 29, though, that the communists eventually fell back from the Long Tieng area.

When the Meo force began its definitive offensive into the Plain of Jars, the cut in American air support had just started. Vang Pao realized that time was not on his side and pushed his forces forward on three axes with speed rather than security his main concern. The communists immediately counterattacked, and between July 7 and 13 two North Vietnamese regiments, supported by PT-76 light tanks, checked the Meo forces and drove them back in some places. The communist pressure continued to increase, and in August the North Vietnamese drove back the Meo column on Route 4, east of the Plain of Jars.

In December, some 15,000 North Vietnamese drove the Meo guerrillas off the Plain of Jars. By December 27, the victorious communist forces had retaken a

number of key points, including the Phou Phaxai and Skyline ridges, on the northern approaches to Long Tieng. As the communist forces bombarded Vang Pao's garrison area with artillery, the rapid evacuation of 30,000 Meo women and children was started.

Back to Normal in Laos?

The artillery bombardment of Vang Pao's headquarters showed that seasonal combat had returned to Laos. The communist forces again, as in previous years, controlled the plateaux, highlands, and Panhandle of Laos, leaving the anticommunist forces in command of the lowlands of the western region. Although the situation had almost traditional aspects, the withdrawal of the South Vietnam from Tchepone and the curtailment of U.S. air support had altered the overall balance of power to a marked degree, and it was clear from the beginning of 1972 that the writing was on

the wall for the anticommunist forces in Laos.

The year 1971 marked the beginning of the eleventh year of U.S. involvement in the Vietnam War. In addition to being the longest war to which the United States had ever been committed, it was also the war that most divided the American people, with the possible exception of the Civil War. By 1971 most Americans felt that the country was exhausted by what they saw as a commitment imposed on it by various presidents, but without any real benefit to the United States.

Most Americans felt that the policy of "Vietnamization" inaugurated by President Nixon was a move in the right direction, for it meant that with the support of some 50,000 Americans, the strengthened South Vietnamese forces would be able to carry the main burden of the war. To the average American, this meant three things: the reduction of American casualties, the extraction of U.S. forces from South Vietnam, and the eventual American disengagement from

Air boats of the type developed for use in the Florida Everglades proved themselves admirably suited to operations in the delta of the Mekong River. Here Sergeant Robert C. Todd, assistant team leader of Detachment A-404, Company "D," 5th Special Forces Group, 1st Special Force, mans the 0·3-inch (7·62-mm) caliber machine gun in the bows of a boat piloted by a student operator of the South Vietnamese Mobile Strike Force.

the war. The other side of the "Vietnamization" coin, however, was an increase in other aspects of U.S. involvement. These were generally presented to the public as measures to make disengagement easier, but were generally seen by the American people as attempts by the administration to broaden U.S. involvement and actually slow the process of disengagement. The American public certainly saw the full-scale commitment of U.S. air power to the Cambodian fighting, a fact revealed to them on January 18, 1971, in this light.

The Communists Strengthen their Hand in South Vietnam

As the American involvement in the land campaign in South Vietnam declined, the communists took advantage of the fact to strengthen their position inside South Vietnam and on the borders. In an attempt to counter, or at least to slow, this buildup, U.S. bombers were launched against communist base areas and movement routes in northwestern South Vietnam and southern Laos at the beginning of 1971 as a prelude to Operation "Lam Son 719 Dewey Canyon II." This operation was, as seen above, not a very good augury for the future ability of South Vietnam to stand on its own two military feet. As part of the effort to prop up the South Vietnamese success in the operation, therefore, President Nixon ordered the bombing of North Vietnamese targets. These missions were flown between April 18 and 23, the heaviest attacks since the "bombing pause" that had come into effect during November 1968.

Festooned with additional belts of machine gun ammunition, men of B Squadron, 3rd Cavalry Regiment, 1st Australian Task Force, 6th Royal Australian Force, move past a bomb crater during a sweep through North Vietnamese bunker complexes south of Ap Rung La in Operation "Mathilda" of 1970.

Notwithstanding the weight of the fighting that was continuing in Southeast Asia, the president announced that the U.S. withdrawal was continuing and was in fact moving ahead more rapidly than proposed by the earlier schedule. On April 26, therefore, there were only 281,000 American service personnel in South Vietnam, well below the figure fixed for May 1 and the lowest total since July 1966. Nixon also said that by December 1 of the same year, U.S. strength would have fallen to 184,000 men. Nixon did not want to be seen as pulling Americans out of South Vietnam without any return, however, and therefore warned North Vietnam to press ahead with solving the problem of returning prisoners-of-war, or face a continued spate of American bombing.

With Operation "Lam Son 719/Dewey Canyon II" over, the intensity of the fighting decreased during the middle part of 1971. In August, the prime ministers of Australia and New Zealand announced that the last of their countries' forces would be pulled out by the end of the year. At the end of 1970, there had been 6,765 Australians (three combat battalions and substantial support elements) and 440 New Zealanders in South Vietnam.

Further Bombing of North Vietnam

Late in September, President Nixon ordered a heavy bombing attack on North Vietnamese forces gathering on the northern side of the Demilitarized Zone with the apparent intention of advancing

The carrierborne air assets of the U.S. Navy operated from the northern "Yankee" and southern "Dixie" stations off the Vietnamese coast. This is the conventionally powered aircraft carrier U.S.S. *Coral Sea* patroling on the "Yankee" Station.

Above: A group of UH-1D helicopters hover above a landing zone.

Right: An infantryman is forced to take cover after being fired upon by a sniper.

Opposite Top: Allied aid for Cambodia arrived by river as well as by land and air. This is part of the South Vietnamese navy dock at Phnom Penh in June 1970.

Opposite Below: The U.S. Air Force's primary on-base rescue helicopter of the 1960s and early 1970s was the twin-rotor Kaman HH-43B Huskie. Here a Huskie uses the downdraft of its rotors to blow a clear path through the smoke burning fuel during at rescue exercise at Korat Air Base in Thailand, one of several such bases used by the U.S. Air Force for operations over Vietnam.

through this prohibited area. Despite a 250-aircraft effort, the war still seemed to be running down, and U.S. forces reported a sharp decrease in their combat activity. This was reflected in the casualty rate, which for the seven days ending on October 9 totaled eight deaths, the lowest weekly total since August 28, 1965. In the following week, the number of combat fatalities dropped to five, and the number of U.S. service personnel in South Vietnam fell to 196,000. President Nixon took advantage of these facts to announce that the U.S. combat involvement in South Vietnam had effectively ended. At the same time, he told the American people that a further 45,000 men would be pulled out of South Vietnam by February 1, 1972, leaving 139,000 Americans, compared with the total of 544,000 men in the country at the time that the withdrawal began on June 15, 1969. Throughout 1970, the rate of withdrawal had been 12,500 Americans each month, rising to 14,300 each month during the second half of 1971.

President Nixon was too politically astute not to cover his own statement, so he also stated that, while the remaining U.S. forces were holding defensive positions, the continued withdrawal depended on three factors: continued North Vietnamese restraint, the success of "Vietnamization," and progress in the talks about prisoner-of-war repatriation. Nixon was under considerable pressure from the Department of Defense, which wanted a speedier withdrawal than then envisaged. The overall vulnerability of the U.S. forces left in South Vietnam was increasing as the troop commitment shrank. By December 1, 1971, the American presence had fallen to 177,000 personnel, some 7,000 less than the president had predicted earlier in the year.

American Media Disbelief

The U.S. media was cynical about the "official line," and reported that the official number should in fact be swelled by the 13,000 or more men on board the ships of the 7th Fleet and by the 32,000 men of the U.S. Air Force per-

sonnel in Thailand, which were both connected directly with the Vietnam War. The media also noted that, while earlier presidential announcements on troop withdrawals had covered several months, the latest covered just a two-month period. This, the media concluded, was intended as yet another warning to the North Vietnamese that the president was determined to forge a direct link between withdrawal and progress in resolving the prisoner-of-war problem.

A Turn for the Worse in Cambodia and Laos

Although the military situation in South Vietnam was satisfactory during December 1971, in the same month it became extremely dangerous in Cambodia and Laos, where communist forces were making serious inroads into the positions held by the government forces. President Nixon was concerned that the policy of "Vietnamization" would be undermined by any collapse of the anticommunist governments of Cambodia and Laos, and on December 26 he ordered the implementation of Operation "Proud Deep Alpha." This was a concentrated attack by U.S. tactical warplanes against North Vietnam's complex of supply and logistical dumps, antiaircraft defenses, and airfields. This short, sharp campaign lasted for five days and was the most crucial escalation of the U.S. air effort since November 1968.

The operation was announced as a package to chastise the North Vietnamese for failing to honor several agreements related to the "bombing pause," the shelling of Saigon, attacks on U.S. reconnaissance aircraft, and violations of the Demilitarized Zone. To the American antiwar movement, however, the operation was the start of a move to prevent a communist advance into the central highlands of South Vietnam, and as such, a tacit admission that "Vietnamization" had failed.

Throughout this period, the "civil war" between President Nixon and the antiwar movement continued. The president claimed that he was moving the inter-

Above: Captain Elbridge G. Fish, II, commanding officer of Troop "F," 2nd Squadron, 11th Armored Cavalry Regiment, orders a reconnaissance by fire to be undertaken by his M113 armored personnel carriers in June 1970.

Opposite: Bell UH-1E "Huey" helicopters of the 1st Marine Air Wing fly in echelon formation over South Vietnam.

ested parties toward an end to the war in Southeast Asia. The antiwar movement counterclaimed that, far from promoting an end to the war, the president had actually increased the level of fighting, and that the only real difference between the war now and before the start of "Vietnamization" was an increase in Asian casualties so that American losses could be reduced. Up to this time, the antiwar movement had been fragmented between factions as far apart as those simply opposed to the Vietnam War and committed pacifists, but from the spring of 1971, the movement began to generate a kind of overall unity. It lost most of the unsympathetic overtones created by its early adherents, most notably revolutionary students and radical politicians, and gained greater credibility as it attracted the endorsement of veteran groups, leaders from a spectrum of political views, the business community, and labor organizations.

American Morale Collapses in South Vietnam

The most notable feature in the revived antiwar movement was the presence of veteran groups, which reflected the plummeting morale of American service personnel left in South Vietnam. This factor was eagerly picked up by the U.S. media, who saw South Vietnam as a hotbed of American corruption (especially among supply personnel), American insensitivity (if not brutality) to the local populations, the practice of "fragging" (the use of fragmentation grenades to kill or maim commissioned and noncommissioned officers considered to be too keen), and drug addiction.

The Drug Problem

This last was perhaps the single greatest

problem. During the 12 months up to June 1966, the authorities investigated 100 drug cases among service personnel in South Vietnam; 96 were found to involve the use of marijuana. By 1967, the number of cases investigated had risen to 1,391, including a far higher percentage involving opium and morphine, and as a result 427 courts-martial were ordered. The problem had continued to escalate, not only in overall numbers, reflecting the increase in the size of the forces in South Vietnam, but in percentage terms. In 1966, the army's worldwide average of drug cases was 0·3 per 1,000 troops, while that in South Vietnam was slightly lower at 0·25. By December 1968, the rate per 1,000 in South Vietnam had risen to 4.5 for marijuana and 0.068 for opium. In 1969, more than 8,000 men were arrested for drug offenses, and this figure rose to 11,058 in 1970, including 1,146 involved with hard drugs. In that year, the army formed a Drug Abuse Task Force, but by 1971 cases involving hard drugs had risen to 7,026 despite the considerable

decrease in the numbers of troops in South Vietnam. It was only in 1972, when force levels fell to a figure below that of 1964, that the problem declined in numerical terms, although in percentage terms, it was still highly worrying.

Larger and Better Organized Demonstrations

The growing strength and impact of the antiwar movement was given added impetus by a demonstration cleverly called Operation "Dewey Canyon III" and launched on April 18, 1971, as an "incursion" into the District of Columbia by an organization called the Vietnam Veterans Against the War. The protest activities of "Dewey Canyon III" caught the public imagination in a major fashion and paved the way for the huge demonstration of April 24 in Washington, DC, and San Francisco, California. Sponsored by the National Peace Action Coalition and the People's Coalition for Peace and Justice, the

The EA-6A electronic warfare platform was a comparatively simple evolution of the Grumman A-6A Intruder carrierborne attack warplane and retained that type's two man crew. The EA-6B Prowler was developed as a fully optimized electronic warfare type for service from 1971.

demonstrations involved 150,000 people in San Francisco and, according to differing sources, between 200,000 and 500,000 people in Washington.

Unlike those of earlier years, the antiwar rallies of 1971 were not one-day demonstrations, but sustained campaigns that lasted until the end of April. These major moves against the war were only the largest and most peaceful of the varied demonstrations, several of which had violent overtones. What was clear, however, was that the American people wanted their troops and their country out of the war. Another wave of demonstrations followed in the fall and early winter, including coordinated rallies in 16 American cities on November 6, with the intention of defeating President Nixon's hopes for re-election in 1972.

The "Pentagon Papers" Debacle

Another major episode of the period was the publication of some of the so-called "Pentagon Papers" in the *New York Times* and later in the *Washington Post*. These "papers" were in fact extracts from an official work, the 47-volume *History of the United States Decision-Making Process on Vietnam Policy* produced in very small numbers (perhaps only 15 sets) in 1968. The work included 3,000 pages of text and 4,000 pages of documentation, and showed clearly that various administrations had first ignored the problem of Southeast Asia, then consistently underestimated the capability of the communists despite warnings, and finally had misled and lied to the American people about what was being done in their name in the war-torn region. The details that were revealed in the press shocked the American people, and the administration tried legal measures to block further publication on the ground that it was a breach of national security. The case eventually reached the Supreme Court, which ruled by a six-to-three majority that publication was in the public interest.

The distrust of the administration engendered by its attempt to suppress

A typical aspect of the Vietnam War is encapsulated in this photograph of men of the 1st Battalion, 9th Cavalry Regiment, 1st Cavalry Division (Airmobile), boarding a Bell UH-1D helicopter in the pick-up zone after a December 1970 sweep.

the "Pentagon Papers" was still high when, in June 1972, the Committee for the Reelection of the President organized the theft of documents from the headquarters of the Democratic Party in Washington's Watergate complex. Seven men were arrested while trying to enter the Democratic Party's offices, and President Nixon was later implicated in efforts to cover up the raid. During August 1974, Nixon was forced to resign, and Vice President Gerald R. Ford took office.

Back in Vietnam, since the military failure of their Tet offensive in February 1968, the communists had been carefully biding their time and building their strength. In the spring of 1972, they felt that the time was ripe for the final offensive that would give them South Vietnam. The resulting Nguyen Hue offensive, also called the Easter invasion or Spring offensive, again failed at the military level. Like the Tet offensive, though, it was a political success when American and international anger at

increased U.S. air and naval intervention nearly caused the United States to abandon South Vietnam to its fate unilaterally.

The offensive also made worse many problems that were already acute or just coming to the boil, including the return of American prisoners-of-war, the doubtful ability of the South Vietnamese forces to hold their country, the presidential demand that the schedule of withdrawal be maintained, and Congressional worry about the financial burden of "Vietnamization." The outcome of the offensive also had ramifications for the negotiations that continued interminably in Paris.

As the time for the Spring offensive approached and it became clear that a major communist effort was in the making, President Nixon was still insisting that troop withdrawals continue, and on May 1, 1972, the American presence in South Vietnam was just 68,200 troops, the lowest figure since 1965.

One of the obsolescent transports that helped create the air bridge between South Vietnam and the west coast of the United States was the piston-engined Douglas C-124 Globemaster II, seen here in the markings of the Oklahoma Air National Guard at Bien Hoa Air Base in August 1970.

The Spring Offensive of 1972

The communist offensive included major efforts in the three most northern of the four corps, tactical zones in South Vietnam. The full extent of the communist aims in the Spring offensive, as in the Tet offensive, remains unknown. The objectives did, however, include a major defeat of the South Vietnamese forces, the dislocation of the "Vietnamization" program, and the overthrow of the South Vietnamese government.

From December 1971, increased movements along the Ho Chi Minh Trail and in the Demilitarized Zone convinced allied intelligence that the communists were planning large-scale offensive action. The basic pattern of

the communist buildup became clearer in January, and allied intelligence anticipated that the communists were planning another Tet offensive. But the Tet holiday passed without incident, and the allies allowed military preparations to lapse. Even so, reconnaissance continued, and among the communist developments that were detected were the grouping of loaded trucks in North Vietnamese supply dumps (apparently awaiting the advent of the dry season to permit extensive movement), the extension of fuel pipelines into the Demilitarized Zone, the building of new surface-to-air missile sites in the southern part of North Vietnam, and extensive deployment of major formations.

During February and March 1972,

allied tactical aircraft, most of them flown by pilots of the South Vietnamese Air Force, undertook numerous sorties against these and other targets. Considerable success was claimed for these attacks, especially as the communists still did not move.

The Battle of Quang Tri

It was just the lull before the storm. On March 30, an artillery barrage across the Demilitarized Zone heralded the beginning of the offensive, as major North Vietnamese infantry formations surged forward behind armored spearheads. The South Vietnamese divisions in the I Corps Tactical Zone in the northernmost Quang Tri province were taken by complete

tactical surprise, and soon the communist forces had taken the South Vietnamese army's most northern fire-support bases. They were of the kind established by the Americans, with artillery to support long-range patrols and hopefully to interdict North Vietnamese encroachments into the Demilitarized Zone, but they had not been planned with a view to local defense against fast-moving enemy forces. The communists therefore took the fire-support bases without difficulty and continued south. The invasion was led by three North Vietnamese divisions, and to the consternation of the defenders, their attackers were supported not just by PT-76 light tanks, but also by elderly but nonetheless effective T-34 medium and more modern T-54 battle tanks. As the invasion continued, moreover, it became clear that the North Vietnamese advance was being supported by mobile surface-to-air missiles (the truck-mounted SA-2 "Guideline" and the portable SA-7 "Grail"), as well as the highly capable 130-mm (5·12-inch) M-46 towed field gun.

The communist attack in Quang Tri province was launched by 40,000 men in three divisions. To meet them, the South Vietnamese also fielded three divisions (including the untested 3rd Infantry Division) which were smaller than their North Vietnamese counterparts; other elements of the South Vietnamese defense were two brigades of marines, and units of the Regional Forces and the Popular Forces. The South Vietnamese divisions were equipped on a lighter scale, and during the crucial early days of the fighting, they suffered a number of catastrophic command and communica-

tion problems. The North Vietnamese had chosen just the right time to attack, for poor weather prevented allied tactical aircraft from attacking them. The South Vietnamese therefore had to rely on naval gunfire from U.S. Navy warships close to the shore, and on area attacks by B-52 Stratofortress heavy bombers operating above the cloud layer and using radar for the navigational data that allowed accurate dropping of their vast loads of conventional "iron" bombs.

After four confused days, the South Vietnamese were able to consolidate along a line between Dong Ha and the Quang Tri combat base. The communists then halted in front of this line, which gave the South Vietnamese the chance to regroup and bring up reinforcements. By April 14, the South Vietnamese had begun to start local offensive actions. Combat operations of this nature remained the norm until April 27,

U.S. Air Force and U.S. Marine Corps personnel unload a Lockheed C-130E Hercules transport against a backdrop of bursting communist shells and mortar bombs.

when the North Vietnamese again struck out under cover of poor weather and took Dong Ha, in the process forcing the South Vietnamese to fall back on the Quang Tri combat base. From this point onward, the South Vietnamese situation began to disintegrate. On April 30, the South Vietnamese decided to abandon the Quang Tri base and, falling back to the south, established a new defensive position centered on the city of Quang Tri. The move to the south was completed during the night, but during May 1, the new line came under heavy fire, and the South Vietnamese defenders, fearing another tank-led infantry attack, broke and began to stream out to the south. One brigade of marines kept its discipline in this worsening rout, but all other units abandoned their tanks, artillery, and even trucks in their panic-stricken flight. The men of the South Vietnamese formations rallied as they headed south, and the

South Vietnamese command was finally able to establish a new defensive line along the southern side of the River Tac Ma. Here the South Vietnamese units regrouped, and preparations were made for a counteroffensive that began in the middle of June.

Hue: Another Objective

The second North Vietnamese thrust was launched on the same day as the first, but farther south against Hue province from Laos. The offensive was directed from the region of the A Shau valley northeast toward the coast and the city of Hue, with the clear objective of cutting off all South Vietnamese forces north of this line. The North Vietnamese drive was at first checked by the South Vietnamese 1st Infantry Division's steadfast defense of the fire-support bases known

as "Bastogne" and "Checkmate." They fell on April 29, and the South Vietnamese then fell back to the "Birmingham" fire-support base to set about creating another defensive block.

It was the major feature of the defense of Hue, and around this bastion the surviving South Vietnamese forces were re-formed and allocated zones of responsibility. The reinforced Marine Division was entrusted with holding the northern and eastern lines of advance on Hue, while the experienced 1st Infantry Division was allocated the task of protecting the southern and western lines of advance. The units of the Regional Forces and the Popular Forces had fought well so far and were grouped under the commander of I Corps as his main reserve. Particular attention was paid to the northwestern and southwestern lines of approach, which were thought to offer the

Men of an armored cavalry regiment "pop" colored smoke grenades as they recross the Cambodian border back into South Vietnam in their M113 armored personnel carriers on June 27, 1970.

communists their best possibilities.

For unknown reasons, the communists did not press their initial advantage in Hue province, which gave the tactical initiative to the South Vietnamese. On May 9, local forces were reinforced by an airborne brigade which had been severely handled in fighting farther south. The brigade was now strengthened by a battalion of artillery and allocated to the Marine Division, which four days later launched a counterattack of brigade size across the River Thac Ma in concert with other local attacks around the Hue defensive perimeter. The South Vietnamese marines also launched a small but useful amphibious attack at the North Vietnamese forces' left flank on May 24.

On May 15, meanwhile, the 1st Infantry Division recaptured "Bastogne" and then moved on to reoccupy "Checkpoint." At this point, the position stabilized and the

Opposite: A man of the 1st Battalion, 9th Cavalry Regiment, 1st Cavalry Division (Airmobile), guides a Bell UH-1D helicopter into the pick-up zone.

Below: Heavily armed men of Troop ''D,'' 1st Squadron, 10th Cavalry Regiment, 4th Infantry Division, board their Bell UH-1D ''Huey'' helicopter in October 1970 after a search-and-clear operation south of Fire Support Base ''Action.''

North Vietnamese, having lost the tactical initiative, were unable to regain it. Throughout the battle, a decisive edge in firepower had been provided to the South Vietnamese by U.S. weapons, most notably the accurate naval guns of American warships and the free-fall ''iron'' bombs that were delivered in vast and devastating numbers by B-52 Stratofortress heavy bombers, which moved in stately and unheard safety far above the effective ceiling of most North Vietnamese antiaircraft weapons.

On June 28, the South Vietnamese went onto the offensive, which had been prepared by intensive artillery fire and bomber attacks, keeping the communists off balance and preventing the arrival of

reinforcements and supplies. Even so, the progress of the South Vietnamese divisions was slow, and it was only on September 16 that the Marine Division recaptured the city of Quang Tri. Thereafter, South Vietnamese operations proceeded slowly and cautiously, but most of the territory lost to the communist Spring offensive was gradually recaptured.

Saigon:
The Main Communist Target

The next component of the Spring offensive was directed through the III corps Tactical Zone from southeastern Cam-

South Vietnamese infantry wait patiently to board their Bell UH-1 "Huey" helicopters for movement into an operational area.

bodia. It had as its initial and final objectives An Loc and Saigon, the latter lying at the heart of the defenses provided by the Capital Special Zone. The communists planned to secure An Loc by April as their capital in South Vietnam, and they grouped one North Vietnamese and two Viet Cong divisions in the border region of Binh Long province.

During March, allied intelligence detected the buildup of communist forces in the III Corps Tactical Zone, but allied commanders came to the conclusion that the offensive effort planned for this area would not be as large as that anticipated farther north. The allied commanders believed that an attempt would be made on Tay Ninh, but thought that the air effort in eastern Cambodia was disrupting communist movement along the Ho Chi Minh Trail so badly that no major threat could be expected. In fact, these commanders had overestimated the effect of the interdiction campaign on the Ho Chi Minh Trail and did not know that the communists had assembled a useful armored force in the region.

The communist offensive got underway on April 1, and the first engagements in the III Corps Tactical Zone happened on the following day when the communists captured the Lac Long fire-support about 22 miles northeast of the city of Tay Ninh. The victorious force was an infantry regiment supported, to the consternation of the allied commanders, by a small but powerful armored force. Then the nearby Thien Ngon fire-support base fell to the communists, and the South Vietnamese command decided that the objective of this thrust was the city of Tay Ninh. Once they reached this conclusion, the South Vietnamese commanders began to alter the placement of their forces to cover this apparent objective. But the move toward Tay Ninh was in fact a feint, which succeeded in drawing off important South Vietnamese units. After their capture of the fire-support bases, however, the communists let an operational gap develop as they limited their activities to patrols in this area.

On April 5, the communists prefaced their attack on An Loc with the capture of Loc Ninh. Held by a South Vietnamese regiment reinforced by an armored cavalry squadron and a ranger battalion, the area was overrun in less than 24 hours, and its defenders suffered virtually total annihilation. Between April

General Alexander M. J. Haig was a major figure in the administration of Richard M. Nixon at the time when the president resigned and was replaced by Vice President Gerald R. Ford.

8 and 12, the communists undertook little in the way of offensive operations. This respite gave the III Corps commander the chance to appreciate that An Loc, rather than Tay Ninh, was the communists' real objective as it would give them access to Route 13 and a clear line of approach to Saigon from the north. Thus the defense of An Loc assumed decisive importance, and reinforcements assigned to the sector included the South Vietnamese 21st Infantry Division and an airborne brigade.

The Battle for An Loc

In the build-up to the battle for An Loc, a South Vietnamese screening force was severely handled about 9 miles north of the city, and in the last five days before the battle itself, there was a great deal of skirmishing. The movement of the communists into their final positions was poorly concealed, and the defenders called for heavy U.S. air support, which included carpet bombing by B-52 Stratofortresses.

The battle itself started on April 13, although the communist effort was badly dislocated by the effect of a B-52 Stratofortress raid on the full depth of the attackers' positions. This phase lasted until April 16, and the full spectrum of air support was employed, with devastating effect, to prevent the communists from taking anything but the northern part of the city and, more unfortunately, the ammunition dump. The first phase of the

A Bell UH-1D helicopter swoops down to collect men of the 75th Infantry Regiment, 25th Infantry Division, after their reconnaissance mission southwest of Xuan Loc in January 1971.

battle did mean that the communists had the city under siege, however, especially after South Vietnamese counterattacks failed to recapture lost ground or to break the communist ring.

In an effort to catch up with their schedule, which demanded the use of An Loc as the capital of the Provisional Revolutionary Government from April 20, the communists resumed their attacks on April 19. The battle continued without respite for some time, and the communists lost large numbers of the armored fighting vehicles used to support their infantry. From April 22, therefore, the battle became an artillery duel rather than an infantry conflict. So dense was the antiaircraft fire put up by the communists, moreover, that not even helicop-

ters could realistically hope to slip into the city. This phase of the battle lasted until May 10, with the communists deluging the defenders with upward of 1,000 rounds of artillery fire a day without gaining any appreciable advantage.

By May 10, the communists had redeployed their seven infantry regiments for a final assault on the city, whose 4,000 defenders now included just under 1,000 wounded men. The communists gave this last attempt to take An Loc everything they could, but the stubborn defense of the South Vietnamese, combined with exceptionally heavy U.S. air attacks, denied them their prize and on May 12, the shattered communists finally fell back as the South Vietnamese 21st Infantry Division and a separate regiment began

One of the more important aircraft allocated to the South Vietnamese Air Force in the "Vietnamization" program was the Cessna A-37B Dragonfly, a light and effective attack warplane. It was derived from the T-37 "Tweet" side-by-side trainer and needed comparatively simple maintenance.

to push in the communist line as they moved to relieve the city. By May 15, the communists had withdrawn their main forces. It was not until June 18 that the siege of An Loc was declared over, however, after South Vietnamese forces had flushed out the last pockets of communist resistance in the area. During the second part of the year, the South Vietnamese gradually drove back the communists and replaced the units that had suffered so heavily in the defense of An Loc.

In the period between April 7 and June 25, An Loc was supplied entirely by air. The supply effort was at first made by allied helicopters and South Vietnamese C-123 Provider aircraft, but it gradually became clear that these slow aircraft were highly vulnerable to the antiaircraft guns that the communists

were massing. Helicopter operations ended on April 12, leaving the C-123s to continue with low-level paradrops until April 19. Thereafter the supply effort was entrusted to the doughty C-130 Hercules, which used low-altitude container drops and high-altitude, low-opening paradrops. Neither delivery method proved particularly successful, and only after the arrival of U.S. air-supply experts did the situation improve, with more than 90 percent of the high-altitude paradrops arriving in the drop zone.

A New Emphasis on the Central Highlands

During the course of the war, there had been considerable fighting in the central

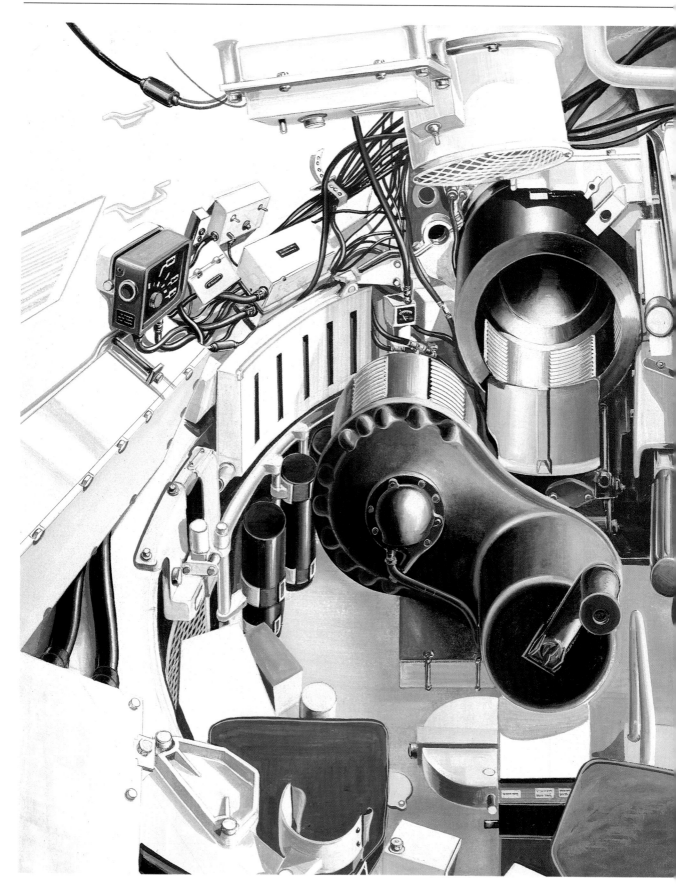

highlands, but nothing to indicate that this region was important in the communists' overall military strategy. From December 1971, though, allied intelligence began to detect clear signs that the communists were gathering strength in the region and fighting small-scale actions with a greater determination. Some intelligence sources then indicated that the communists were planning a three-phase offensive in the central highlands during February. During January, aerial reconnaissance indicated that North Vietnamese tanks were moving into the area, but these indications received no ground confirmation and were generally disregarded. Even so, it seemed prudent to reinforce the area as other reports indicated that the communists were moving 122- and 130-mm (4·8- and 5·12-inch) artillery into the border region. During February, therefore, the South Vietnamese reinforced their units in the central highlands with some armor and one brigade of the Airborne Division, which was used to strengthen the defenses of the important fire-support bases on "Rocket Ridge," west of the city of Kontum. Early in March, South Vietnamese preparations were completed by the arrival of the rest of the Airborne Division, which was entrusted with the defense of Kontum and the south of Kontum province.

Throughout this period, the communists were massing two infantry divisions in the area, but the extent and scheduling of their program was seriously affected by U.S. air power, which again used carpet bombing by B-52 Stratofortresses and point attacks by tactical warplanes to inflict heavy personnel casualties and materiel losses on the communists. Over the same period, contact on the ground between the two sides increased, and the early skirmishing soon gave way to larger and harder-fought actions.

By April 23, the communists were finally ready, and launched their central highlands offensive with an initial move against Tan Canh on Route 14, covering the northern approaches to Kontum. The communists took the "Charlie" and "Delta" fire-support bases on "Rocket Ridge" overlooking Route 14 from the

Previous Page: This artwork shows the inside of a light tank, the M551 Sheridan. Its most unusual feature was the 152-mm (6-inch) caliber gun, designed to fire low-velocity shells or, in the antitank role, Shillelagh missiles.

Above: Seen at Dong Ha Air Base in February 1971, this U.S. Air Force Lockheed C-130 Hercules transport was awaiting its unloading crew during Operation "Dewey Canyon II," the American part of the offensive leading to the incursion into Laos.

west, and the South Vietnamese responded by strengthening the defense of Tan Canh. From their new positions, the communists were able to dominate the area with their artillery, and by April 24 the South Vietnamese were finding that their M41 light tanks were being targeted by direct fire. That day, the communists attacked Tan Canh, and by midday had destroyed the command bunker and all five of the defenders' tanks. The morale of the Tan Canh defenders was low, for they did not react to the communist attacks and, when the ammunition dump was destroyed in the evening, the South Vietnamese took to their bunkers. On the following day, a North Vietnamese armor-spearheaded attack developed, and the 900 men of the South Vietnamese regiment garrisoning the area broke and streamed away to the rear, giving Tan Canh to the communists.

Over the same period, the communists attacked another regimental headquarters and the airfield at Dak To II South Vietnamese armor made a counterattack on April 24, but the defenders

soon broke and effectively gave the position to the communists.

The loss of these two key positions forced the South Vietnamese to reorganize the defense of Kontum, and a particularly unfortunate result was the subordination of several colonels to an officer of the same rank, who thus found it difficult to enforce his authority. Further problems were caused by the loss of the "November" fire-support base just north of the city on May 4, and the effective neutralization of the South Vietnamese ranger camps west of the city, whose garrisons might otherwise have disrupted the communist lines of communication. The main weight of these attacks was directed against the camps at Ben Het and Polei Kleng, and while the former remained, the latter was bludgeoned into surrender.

The Battle for Kontum

The attack of Kontum began on May 14, with attacks from the northwest and

Previous Page: This underside view of three McDonnell Douglas F-4D Phantom II multirole fighters of the 8th Tactical Fighter Wing in September 1972 reveals a miscellany of equipment. All three aircraft carry AIM-7 Sparrow medium-range air-to-air missiles, the two aircraft in the foreground also carry "Paveway" laser-guided bombs, and the third fighter sports guidance equipment for the "Paveways." With precision weapons such as the "Paveway" available late in the war, the U.S. Air Force was finally able to destroy point targets that had long defied the efforts of aircraft carrying only conventional weapons.

Above: A tactical warplane used by the U.S. Navy and U.S. Air Force was the Vought A-7, a comparatively simple but effective subsonic warplane that was based on the aerodynamics of the F-8 Crusader supersonic fighter. The naval versions are called the Corsair II, but the air force models have no name. These are A-7Ds of the 354th Tactical Fighter Wing, which transferred from Myrtle Beach Air Force Base, South Carolina, to Korat Air Base in Thailand during October 1972.

Colonel Arthur D. "Bull" Simons, the commander of the Son Tay raid, rides with his wife in an open car during an April 1973 parade through the financial district of San Francisco.

One of the aircraft supplied to the South Vietnamese Air Force after limited operational use by the U.S. Air Force was the Northrop F-5A Freedom Fighter single-seat maintenance capabilities. The Freedom Fighter first flew specially designed without radar to be used by American allies with limited resources and limited bases and maintenance capabilities. The Freedom Fighter first flew in July 1959 with the first deliveries made in October 1963.

Right: General Robert E. Cushman, Jr., commandant of the U.S. Marine Corps, takes a ride with Gunnery Sergeant C. M. Hallman of the corps' Schools Division, in the new M561 rough-terrain cargo vehicle, generally known as the Gama Goat. The place was the Marine Corps Supply Center at Albany, Georgia, and the date November 1972.

Below: A view of the S.S. *Green Bay* in a South Vietnamese harbor after a 500-pound explosive charge had been exploded against her hull by the Viet Cong in October 1971.

north spearheaded by T-54 battle tanks. Air support proved a decisive weapon, and by the middle of the morning, the communist attack had been checked by tactical warplanes and AH-1 HueyCobra helicopter gunships. A considerable toll of communist tanks was also taken by South Vietnamese infantrymen equipped with the rocket-launching weapon known as the M72 LAW (Light Antitank Weapon). Even so, the communists broke through the South Vietnamese defense in several places, and it was the evening before the South Vietnamese restored the integrity of their defensive positions in savage hand-to-hand fighting. The communists attacked again in the early part of the night and again broke through. Fearing that they would be unable to stem this communist breakthrough, the South Vietnamese fell back, and B-52 Stratofortress bombers devastated the positions that had been overrun, thereby checking the communist advance.

A two-day interval ended with the beginning of a communist artillery bombardment. On May 20, the South Vietnamese again came under attack, and

Right: The M50 Ontos was designed as an antitank vehicle with six 106-mm (4.17-inch) caliber recoilless rifles, but it was widely used by the marine corps in the Vietnam War as a fire-support vehicle.

Below: Men of the 151st (Ranger) Infantry Long Range Patrol open fire on a communist position with their 5.56-mm (0.219-inch) caliber M16A1 assault rifles.

while some of the defenders broke, the majority held their positions and checked the communists. Another attack developed on May 21, and again the defenders beat back the communists with the aid of tactical support from B-52 Stratofortress bombers.

Another lull followed, and during this time the South Vietnamese launched some local counterattacks to restore their positions. The communists were not yet beaten, however, and on May 25 they launched another major effort. This time, the South Vietnamese were unable to prevent communist breakthroughs on a larger scale. The defense called for emergency air support of the greatest possible weight, and over the next few days, this played a key part in preventing the loss of Kontum. During the night of May 25-26, the communists drove a wedge between two South Vietnamese regiments, but in the morning, their supporting tanks were caught in the open by AH-1 HueyCobra gunships, whose TOW antitank missiles destroyed the North Vietnamese armor.

During the day, South Vietnamese reinforcements arrived, but the situation remained critical until May 30. On that day, President Thieu visited his men to boost their morale and urge on them the importance of holding Kontum. A more positive move was the promotion of the commanding colonel to brigadier general, thereby easing the command situation. This was the decisive moment in the battle for Kontum; on May 31, it became clear that the communists could do no more and were now beginning to pull back to avoid the possibility of encirclement by the South Vietnamese counteroffensive that was getting underway.

As the battle for Kontum raged, a North Vietnamese division was fighting with the support of Viet Cong main force units in operations along the coast of Binh Dinh province farther to the east. This was another part of the communists' overall plan, for the capture of Kontum, Pleiku, and Binh Dinh provinces would have cut South Vietnam in two, severing the eight northern most provinces and the South Vietnamese I Corps from the rest of the country. The communists succeeded in cutting Route

1 and capturing several district capitals, but an increasingly steady defense and U.S. tactical air power prevented the communists from gaining any real success along the coast.

So the Spring offensive ended. The communists had made considerable inroads, but again the South Vietnamese had rallied and with the aid of U.S. air support had checked the communist advances. Fighting continued during the rest of the year as the South Vietnamese launched a series of counteroffensives that eroded the areas of South Vietnam held by the communists.

Strategic Air War against North Vietnam

In parallel with the tactical air support provided by American aircraft to the South Vietnamese ground forces, there was also a resumption of the strategic air war against North Vietnam. This campaign started on April 12, when B-52 made their first attacks on North Vietnamese targets since November 1967. The importance attached to the campaign became clear just five days later, when American aircraft made very heavy attacks on targets of military importance in the area of Hanoi and Haiphong, respectively the capital and most important port of North Vietnam. To the countries of the communist bloc, this was "evidence" that the United States was once more trying to escalate the war, and this sentiment was echoed with increasingly virulence by the antiwar movement within the United States. All over the country, hundreds of antiwar demonstrations erupted, and the Democratic candidates in the forthcoming presidential elections condemned the bombing campaign as an unjustifiable way to check the communist invasion of South Vietnam and force the communists into meaningful negotiations at Paris. The task of answering these points fell to Secretary of Defense Melvin R. Laird, who on April 18 said that the United States had been "very restrained" up to this time, but had been "answered by an invasion" through the Demilitarized Zone (and also from Laos and Cambodia) in a completely flagrant disregard of the 1968

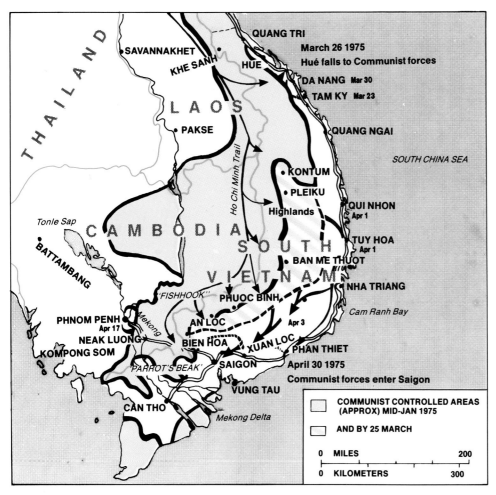

The North Vietnamese deployment on the eve of the offensive that ended South Vietnam iis existence as a nation in spring 1975.

agreement that had ended the earlier bombing of North Vietnam.

The United States maintained the offensive against North Vietnam until the end of 1972, with the efforts of the air forces supplemented by gunfire from warships. The intensity of the campaign waxed and waned, and its main objectives were a number of military targets, as well as military-associated features such as power generating plants, factories, and bridges. Such attacks inevitably killed civilians, and this increasingly became the main accusation leveled at the United States, together with the destruction of nonmilitary targets such as the dikes that controlled the level of the water in North Vietnam's waterways and irrigation system.

On May 8, President Nixon authorized the mining of Haiphong and six other North Vietnamese ports used by ships bringing in war supplies. This move added further to the opprobrium heaped on the United States by the opposition, both domestic and international. By the middle of October, progress in the Paris negotiations indicated that a ceasefire was imminent, and on October 23 the president forbade bombing north of the 20th parallel. With this objective secured, the communists then reverted to their former intransigence, and on December 18 the president authorized Operation "Linebacker II" for the heaviest bombing of the entire war. American aircraft achieved total air superiority over North Vietnam and inflicted very heavy damage on North Vietnam's war-making capabilities and economic infrastructure. International and domestic opposition once again rose, but the communists started practical negotiations again. On December 30, Nixon again halted the bombing of targets north of the 20th parallel.

Throughout this period, the American disengagement continued as troop levels continued to fall to 96,000 by March 31, 32,000 by October 31, and 24,000 by December 31.

Continued Talking in Paris

Throughout 1972, the negotiations in Paris continued. The formal talks were paralleled by informal discussions between Dr. Henry A. Kissinger, Nixon's national security adviser, and Le Duc Tho, the North Vietnamese chief negotiator. Despite the rhetoric of the talks, in which each side accused the other, among other things, of dishonesty, changing demands, and failure to fulfill promises, some

progress was made – if only in the clarification of each side's negotiating position. The United States wanted to make sure that South Vietnam had at least a chance to maintain its independence through elections and to secure the release of prisoners-of-war within any agreement for American withdrawal; North Vietnam wanted a new government in South Vietnam and called for the resignation of the Thieu administration in favor of a coalition government.

A Ceasefire Ends American Involvement

On October 26, Kissinger revealed his belief that ''peace is at hand.'' The North

A Vought A-7E Corsair II attack warplane of the VA-97 squadron taxis on the deck of the nuclear-powered aircraft carrier U.S.S. Enterprise during the period in April 1975 when the carrier's aircraft covered the evacuation of American and selected South Vietnamese personnel from Saigon.

Dr. Henry Kissinger and Le Duc Tho, head of the American and North Vietnamese delegations, initial the agreement that ended the Paris peace talks, but not the Vietnam War.

Vietnamese then returned to their stalling tactics, which was one of the reasons for "Linebacker II." One of the reasons for this operation's termination was an agreement on December 30 that meaningful negotiation would be resumed in open negotiation and private discussion. These talks finally produced a ceasefire initialed by Kissinger and Tho on January 23, 1973, before final signature four days later on January 27. The last stage of the American withdrawal then began, and North Vietnam released those American and South Vietnamese prisoners-of-war it admitted it was holding. Nixon announced that this was a settlement that brought "peace with honor," and most Americans agreed with this sentiment.

What the settlement achieved was the final American disengagement from the Vietnam War. What it did not address was the fact that about 33 percent of South Vietnam's territory and about 5 percent of its population were controlled by communist forces totaling 145,000 men. The South Vietnamese forces continued a low-key war in an effort to expel the communists, but they lacked the strength and air power to strike decisive blows. The communists were therefore able to develop roads, garrisons, supply dumps, and even an airfield in the area they held, biding their time for a final offensive when the political situation in the United States would make American re-involvement impossible, despite the assurances given by Nixon to Thieu in order to secure South Vietnamese approval of the January 1973 ceasefire.

When the last American prisoners-of-war were released, the headquarters of the Military Assistance Command, Vietnam, were relocated to Nakhon Phanom in Thailand and became the headquarters of the U.S. Support Activities Group. The American presence in South Vietnam was the Saigon-based Defense Attache Office, made up mainly of civilians. In the United States, the antiwar movement and its Congressional supporters now turned their attentions to ending the military assistance still being supplied to South Vietnam. In October 1974, Congress voted only $700 million for military assistance to the South Vietnamese forces, $300 million below the

The North Vietnamese offensive of March and April 1975 secured unexpected success and at last ended the Vietnam War.

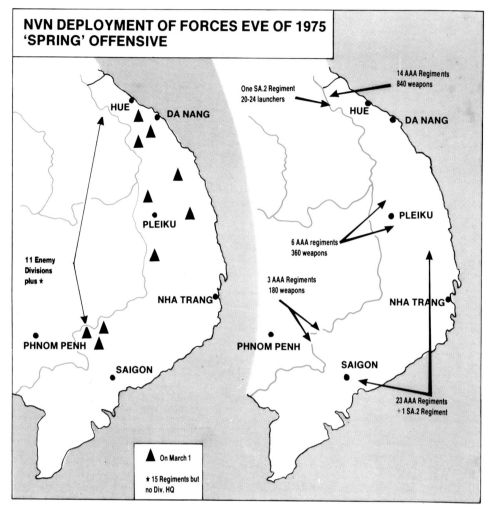

NVN DEPLOYMENT OF FORCES EVE OF 1975 'SPRING' OFFENSIVE

14 AAA Regiments 840 weapons

One SA.2 Regiment 20-24 launchers

HUE

DA NANG

6 AAA regiments 360 weapons

PLEIKU

3 AAA Regiments 180 weapons

NHA TRANG

11 Enemy Divisions plus ★

PLEIKU

PHNOM PENH

SAIGON

23 AAA Regiments + 1 SA.2 Regiment

▲ On March 1

★ 15 Regiments but no Div. HQ

Below: A U.S. armored troop carrier (ATC) answers a Vietcong sniper fire with a blast from the flame thrower located in its well deck.

benchmark figure that had been used only recently to establish aid levels. This cut clearly showed that continued American support would be very limited. The morale of South Vietnam was badly hit, and in physical terms, it meant the disbanding of 11 out of 66 South Vietnamese air force squadrons, as well as a drastic reduction in the number of flying hours permitted to the surviving 55 squadrons. As air power was the major weapon in keeping the communists in check, this blow to the chances of South Vietnam's survival was enormous.

The Communists Consolidate Their Grip

The communists continued to consolidate and strengthen their position in South Vietnam and to exert more pressure on the beleaguered position of Lon Nol in Cam-

A South Vietnamese-marked Bell UH-1 ''Huey'' goes over the side of an American warship to make room for other helicopters to touch down with their loads of fleeing South Vietnamese.

bodia. American air support for Lon Nol ended on August 15, 1973, and from January 1975, the communists started the effort that gave them total control of the country by April 16, 1975, just four days after helicopters of the U.S. Marine Corps lifted out a final 276 Americans from a field near the American embassy in Phnom Penh. Cambodia and its hapless population were now at the mercy of the murderous regime of Pol Pot.

Communist strength in South Vietnam increased to 300,000 men by late 1974, and these forces were grouped in the border regions flanking Cambodia and Laos, which gave them interior lines of communication and thus a distinct operational advantage over the South Vietnamese forces. From this time, the communists slowly expanded their area of control into provinces neighboring their core area. At the same time, the North Vietnamese government approved a two-year plan designed to conquer South Vietnam by the end of 1976. The plan envisaged a major offensive in 1975, paving the way for a general offensive and a communist uprising that would topple the regime of President Thieu in 1976.

The End for South Vietnam

In December 1974, the communists attacked and overran Phuoc Long province. The South Vietnamese government decided to abandon the highlands and the coastal strip it still held in the north, instead pulling back its forces to hold Saigon and the southern part of the country. The retreat turned into a rout, and the pursuing communists took Hue on March 26, 1975, with Da Nang following on March 30, and both Qui Nhon and Tuy Hoa on April 1. The last combat-capable South Vietnamese forces made a last stand at Xuan Loc, 40 miles northeast of Saigon, but were driven back after a week. This left only three divisions to hold Saigon against the rampant

Above Left: A "Huey" helicopter of the South Vietnamese forces goes down after being thrown over the side of the amphibious command ship U.S.S. *Blue Ridge* on April 28, 1975, to make room for further arrivals.

Above Right: South Vietnamese small craft line up to have their loads of refugees taken on board the amphibious cargo ship U.S.S. *Durham* in 1975. Such boatloads are still happening, more than 15 years after the end of the Vietnam War, as Vietnamese try to flee the country.

Right: A ferry carries passengers and vehicles across a Vietnamese river. A high proportion of the men are soldiers of the Vietnamese Army.

Right: Scars caused by 30 years of war. Playgrounds still feature mounds of rusting artillery projectiles amid bullet-pocked buildings.

Below: The end of U.S. involvement in the Vietnam War resulted in the release of 588 prisoners of war. Here Captain James D. Kula is greeted by the American delegation at Hanoi's Gia Lam Airport after his release from a North Vietnamese camp. Yet, even in the early 1990s, there remain doubts that the communists have returned all American prisoners.

communist forces, and the war ended on April 30 when the communist forces entered Saigon.

President Thieu had resigned on April 21. Announcing the fact in a television broadcast, he attacked the United States for its abandonment of South Vietnam and revealed the promises of support made to South Vietnam by Nixon and now thoroughly broken. The last act of this terrible war was Operation "Frequent Wind," in which a fleet of helicopters flew refugees out to ships of the 7th Fleet in the South China Sea. The effort rescued 1,373 American civilians, 6,422 non-Americans, and 989 men of the U.S. Marine Corps who had been lifted ashore at the beginning of the operation to protect the landing site.

So the involvement of the United States with the Vietnam War ended, even though the conflict in Southeast Asia still had a considerable course to run before major operations ended.

Glossary

Aircraft carrier The type of warship that took over from the battleship as the world's most important type of capital ship during World War II. It is in essence a floating airfield with provision for hangaring, maintaining, and operating a substantial number of aircraft.

Armored personnel carrier A vehicle designed to move troops on the battlefield. It is generally a tracked vehicle that provides the embarked men protection against small arms fire; the troops are generally carried in a compartment at the rear of the vehicle accessed, in the case of the American M113, by a powered rear ramp/door.

Artillery An overall term for tube weapons that fire shells rather than bullets, and which are too large and complex to be operated by an individual soldier.

Battalion A basic subdivision of the regiment, generally less than 1,000 men and commanded by a lieutenant colonel.

Blockade A naval and/or air campaign to deny the enemy or neutrals access to or departure from the enemy's ports and coast.

Bomber An airplane designed to deliver free-fall bombs, therefore a comparatively large type with greater range than the fighter. It generally carries its offensive weapons in a lower-fuselage bomb bay and is fitted with defensive gun turrets to deal with enemy fighters.

Brigade The basic subdivision of a division, generally containing two or more battalions and commanded by a brigadier general.

Company The basic subdivision of a battalion, generally less than 200 men and commanded by a captain. The cavalry equivalent is the troop.

Corps A primary component of the army containing two or more divisions. A corps is commanded in the U.S. Army by a major general, but in most other armies by a lieutenant general.

Destroyer A warship intermediate in size and capability between a frigate and a cruiser. The type is one of any navy's "workhorse" vessels which combines affordability with high performance, and it is large enough to carry a useful sensor and weapon load.

Division The smallest army formation, including two or more brigades and commanded by a major general. It is the basic organization designed for independent operation and therefore contains support elements (artillery, engineers, etc.) in addition to its infantry.

Formation Any large body of troops organized for operations independent of the rest of the army. It therefore possesses, in addition to its organic infantry units, a full complement of artillery, engineer, and support services. The smallest formation is generally the division.

Gun One of the basic weapons of the artillery. It is a high-velocity weapon with a comparatively long barrel designed for the direct engagement (firing at an elevation angle below 45°) of targets that can be seen through the weapon's sight.

Howitzer One of the basic weapons of the artillery. It is a low-velocity weapon with a comparatively short barrel, designed for the indirect engagement (firing at an elevation angle of more than 45°) of targets hidden from direct sight by some intervening feature.

Logistics The science of planning and carrying out the movement of forces and their supplies.

Materiel The overall term for equipment, stores, supplies, and spares.

Regiment A basic tactical unit, subordinate to the brigade and made up of two or more battalions under the command of a colonel.

Mine An explosive device generally encased in metal or plastic and designed to destroy or incapacitate vehicles, or to kill or wound personnel. The two basic types of mine are the land mine, a comparatively small weapon which is usually buried in the ground, and the sea mine, a considerably larger weapon either laid on the bottom of shallow waters or, in deeper waters, floating just below the surface at the top of an anchored cable.

Mortar A light tube weapon, made up of a barrel, supporting leg(s), and a baseplate. It can be broken down into sections to be hand carried and is designed to fire its bombs on a high trajectory that ends with an almost vertical descent on the target.

Recoilless rifle An antitank (and antibunker) weapon that generates no recoil as it fires a rocket-powered projectile.

Strategy The art of winning a campaign or war by major operations.

Tactics The art of winning a battle by minor operations.

Unit Any small body of troops not organized with capability for operations independent of the rest of the army. Therefore, it does not possess in addition to its organic infantry units the full range of artillery, engineer, and support services. The largest unit is the regimental combat team, generally known in other armies as the brigade.

Bibliography

Arnold, James R. *Armor.*
(Bantam Books, New York, 1987).
The surprising usefulness of armored fighting vehicles in Vietnam.

Arnold, James R. *Rangers.*
(Bantam Books, New York, 1988).
The specially trained recon forces and superior ARVN Rangers battalions.

Boettcher, Thomas D. *Vietnam: The Valor and the Sorrow.*
(Little, Brown & Co., Boston, 1985).

Broughton, Jack. *Thud Ridge.*
(Bantam Books, New York, 1985).
A pilot's account of aerial combat over North Vietnam.

Brown, Malcolm W. *The New Face of War.*
(Bantam Books, New York, 1986).

Caputo, Philip. *A Rumor of War.*
(Holt Rinehart & Winston, New York, 1977).

Donovan, David. *Once A Warrior King: Memories of an Officer in Vietnam.*
(McGraw-Hill, New York, 1985).
An advisor's story who served in an isolated post in the Delta.

Fall, Bernard. *Street Without Joy.*
(The Stackpole Company, Harrisburg PA, 1967).
Primarily focused on the French in Indochina; essential for understanding what befell the U.S.

Giap, Vo Nguyen. *Big Victory, Great Task.*
(Frederick A. Praeger, New York, 1968).
By the strategic genius behind the North Vietnamese war effort.

Goldman, Peter and Tony Fuller et. al. *Charlie Company: What Vietnam Did to Us.*
(William Morrow & Co., New York, 1983).

Hackworth, David H., and Julie Sherman. *About Face: The Odyssey of an American Warrior.*
(Simon & Schuster, New York, 1989).
The story of the disillusionment of a crack warrior.

Henderson, Charles. *Marine Sniper.*
(Stein & Day, New York, 1986).
The amazing exploits of a master marksman.

Knoebl, Kuno. *Victor Charlie: The Face of War in Vietnam.*
(Frederick A. Praeger, New York, 1967).

Mason, Robert. *Chickenhawk.*
(Penguin Books, New York, 1984).
The helicopter war.

Maurer, Harry. *Strange Ground: Americans in Vietnam 1945-1975.*
(Henry Holt & Co, New York, 1989).
Excellent compilation of oral histories from soldiers at all levels.

Oberdorfer, Don. *Tet!*
(Doubleday & Co., Garden City, NY, 1971).

Santoli, Al. *Everything We Had: An Oral History of the Vietnam War by Thirty-Three American Soldiers Who Fought There.*
(Random House, New York, 1981).
Excellent compilation of first-hand accounts.

Sheehan, Neil. *A Bright Shining Lie.*
(Random House, New York, 1988).
A massive, detailed account about a very influential American adviser to South Vietnam.

Stanton, Shelby L. *Anatomy of a Division: 1st Cav in Vietnam.*
(Presidio Press, Novato, CA, 1987).
An organizational and battle history of the world's first air cavalry division.

Summers, Col. Harry G., Jr. *On Strategy: The Vietnam War in Context.*
(U.S. Army War College, Carlisle, PA, 1981).
A controversial description of what went wrong, focusing on the strategic level.

Walt, Lewis W. *Strange War, Strange Strategy: A General's Report on Vietnam.*
(Funk & Wagnalls, New York, 1970).
A respected Marine Corps general's war memoirs.

Westmoreland, Gen. William C. *A Soldier Reports.*
(Doubleday & Co., Garden City, NY, 1976).
Top American commander's war memoirs.

Index

Page numbers in *Italics* refer to illustration